THE
EVOLUTION
OF
MANAGEMENT
THEORY

PAST, PRESENT, FUTURE

William Roth

Roth & Associates
Orefield, Pennslyvania

Published By Roth & Associates
6223 Hilltop Road,
Orefield, PA 18069
(215) 395-3449
(215) 395-3604 FAX

Design & Production by Farley Printing Company, Inc.,
   Wilmington, Delaware

9 8 7 6 5 4 3 2 1
FIRST EDITION

ISBN 0-9635680-1-9   Library of Congress No. 93-92548

Printed in the U.S.A.

THE EVOLUTION OF MANAGEMENT THEORY

Contents

Introduction
Foreword
Acknowledgments

Bibliography
Index

INTRODUCTION

Organizations today are struggling to make their management systems more effective. Most are losing the battle. Part of the problem is that they do not understand the evolving nature of these systems. They do not understand the forces that have shaped them historically, that are currently shaping them, and that will shape them in the future. Without such understanding, efforts are too often blind and fragmented.

The Evolution of Management Theory explores modern day management practices, attitudes, and values. It begins with their origins, showing how many of these practices are rooted in much earlier periods — the Medieval Era, the Renaissance, the Reformation, the Early Industrial Revolution — and have changed little as the centuries rolled on, though the world being managed has changed radically.

Our journey through time will be framed in terms of four interdependent, history-shaping forces:

1) Socio-Economic Thinking — What effects have social and economic thinking had on management systems historically? What affects have changes in this thinking had? Have teachers in both schools and churches encouraged a cooperative, competitive, or conflict ethic in the workplace? How and why has this ethic changed? How and why should it change?

2) Technological Development — What have been the effects of technological development on management processes historically? Has increased technological sophistication led to increased or decreased employee involvement? Is technology itself currently capable of taking over at least some traditional management responsibilities?

3) Organization Size — How have changes in business

size affected organization design and management systems? What problems does growth present? Are the requirements for effective management themselves a constraint to growth beyond a certain point? What lessons can we learn from the past concerning organization size and design? What design characteristics will be necessary to success in the future?

4) Marketplace Pleasures—What have been the effects of marketplace pressures on management systems? As competition and demand have both increased, how have these systems adapted?

The book will show how the importance of these four forces has peaked and ebbed in an on-going cycle, and how, in terms of modern day management trends, we are in some ways back to where we started. The book will explore key historic moments—birth of the profit motive and the Protestant Work Ethic, the rise of mass production, the factory, laissez-faire economics, domination of the robber barons advent of the union movement, the involvement of academia, the humanist movement, scientific management, global competition, the computer, systems theory, the quality improvement movement.

The book will discuss the fact that we are close to turning another historic corner, not in terms of technology this time, though technology has certainly helped us get there, but in terms of the individual and societal values upon which management theory and practices are based. It will also discuss the dangers spawned by our progress, most resulting from the lack of a true understanding of the big picture. It will discuss the fact that we are currently trying to deal with these dangers piecemeal, but cannot do so successfully because they are systemic in nature and centuries in the making.

Our challenge, then, if we want to get around that corner, is to develop a new way of thinking. Fortunately, as so frequently occurs in history, the necessary vehicle has materialized. In this case it is the quality improvement movement. The book will discuss briefly the nature of that movement.

FORWARD

William Roth has written a unique book about the history of management — past, present, future. Though the ground covered is immense, the book is admirably brief and the writing style so direct that the general reader should have no difficulty in understanding the concepts and methods presented, many of which are sophisticated.

Most books of this kind are written for students taking graduate level courses, or for managers with an MBA background. While Roth's book should have a high place on the reading lists of these audiences because of the various perspectives it brings together, it has a far wider appeal because of its brevity and directness. I recommend it not only for undergraduate courses at the university level, but for high school seniors as well.

We have reached a stage in our complex and rapidly changing society where management has become as much an art as a science. A book such as The Evolution of Management Theory which shows how this circumstance came about and where it is leading us is of great value to all those interested in improving their quality of work life, and their quality of life in general.

Eric Trist
Professor Emeritus
The Wharton School
University of Pennsylvania

ACKNOWLEDGMENTS

A book like this is based on the contributions and support of a lot of people. It's hard to acknowledge them all. In my case, the most important are the men who taught me at The Wharton School. Thanks to Eric Trist, who brought me into the doctoral program and continues to provide a role model for completeness and humility. Thanks to Russell Ackoff, whose vision and desire were largely responsible for the systems based program I earned my degree in and whose relentless quest for exactness has fine honed the mind of many a stumbling student. Thanks to Hasan Ozbekhan, who functioned as my spiritual guide and friend during those years. Thanks to Jamshid Gharajedaghi, who took me in tow at a critical stage of my education and helped me put the pieces together in a way that made sense. And finally, thanks to Fred Emery, who arrived late upon the scene, but made a strong, positive impression on my work and views.

A second category of those I must thank begins with a progressive and truly humanistic academic institution, Allentown College St. Francis de Sales. The administration and faculty there have offered a remarkable amount of support and encouragement to my efforts. Individual thanks go to Fr. Gambet, the president of Allentown College, who made it all possible. Hal Dolenga, my special friend, and the rest of the Department of Business faculty.

A third category includes those who never have allowed me to doubt that I am capable of making a contribution – Pat Brandt and Joan Lonetti, Stephanie Olen, Omid Nodoushani, Ali Geranmayeh, John Kalish, Doug and Susan Ferguson, Ned Hamson, Pete Grazier, Uncle Fred, my darling wife Wendy, my two well-loved sons, Ian and Dane, and finally my two four-legged walk-through-the-woods-and think companions, Jessy and Ricki.

1

The Pre-Industrial Revolution Era

MANAGEMENT PRACTICES DURING THE MEDIEVAL PERIOD

The pre-Industrial Revolution era can be divided into three periods the Medieval period, the Renaissance period, and the Reformation period. During the Medieval period of European history guilds were organized to control both the production and distribution of goods. A "guild" was an association of businessmen engaged in a common trade which was formed to regulate that trade. The main responsibilities of the guild were to protect the interests of member units from outside competition and to restrain these units from taking unfair advantage of each other. Guilds also controlled the training of apprentices and limited the number of craftsmen producing goods for the local marketplace.

While guild-controlled craftsmen had no social mobility,

almost no geographical mobility, and little chance to improve their economic situation, they generally had job security. Man during this period was not an individual with potential and competitive drives. Rather, he was a member of a closely knit community, his efforts contributing to the advancement of the whole. The real business of life was not to increase wealth. Instead, it was to gain salvation through unselfish acts. Economic conduct, as well as personal conduct, were bounded by the rules of morality and, to a large degree, by the laws of the church, which housed God's representatives on earth. Business profits, therefore, when any existed, were used mainly to glorify God and do good works in his name.

Businesses were typically hierarchical in structure. Staffs were composed of owner/bosses called "master craftsmen" who participated in production as well as management, "journeymen," and "apprentices." This structure mirrored the structure of church and state. The management philosophy of business, however, did not mirror that of church and state. Church parishioners and state subjects on one hand were children to be controlled, guided, and taken care of. They were expected to contribute when called upon without question, but were allowed little input into the management process. On the other hand, while business employees were to be controlled, guided, and taken care of, they were, unlike parishioners and subjects, also expected to contribute to the solution of problems. At least the problem solving part of management during this period, therefore, was a group exercise.

The above defined situation existed for several reasons. First, guild-controlled businesses were relatively small and served mainly local populations. Each offered an extremely limited variety of products, frequently only one. This was due partially to the fact that relatively few "products" existed. Technical systems were limited by a lack of appropriate research. This, combined with a lack of communication technology, made the development of new products sporadic and uncoordinated. Such smallness of operational size and simplicity of technology, however, facilitated participation in the management process. Those who controlled the organization's social system (that involving employees/people rather than technology/machines) knew the expertise of all employees and could utilize that expertise advantageously. Inputs could be gathered and a consensus shaped without slowing production unacceptably.

Second, guilds encouraged craftsmen to share innovations and to pass knowledge on to apprentices. Guild training programs turned out new craftsmen familiar with every aspect of the item produced. Local sales were often made directly from producer to customer with no middlemen involved. Therefore, workers could take part in all phases of the business planning, production, sales along with the owner-boss and frequently the customer. Gaining the necessary overview from such total involvement, they could make meaningful contributions.

Third, utilization of employee expertise in decision making situations was facilitated by the fact that an adversary relationship had not yet formed between management and labor. The ethic that guided boss/employee relationships was cooperation. "Cooperation" occurs when boss/employee "A"'s efforts increases boss/employee "B"'s chances of fulfilling his work related needs/desires, and vice versa. Management was frequently involved directly in production and, therefore functioned as part of labor. Also, because of the "family" nature of early businesses and business-guild relationships, grievances could be worked out informally and immediately within the organization's social system.

The church provided the "family" model. Church leaders were benevolently paternalistic. Business leaders strove to emulate this model in order to gain grace. Finally, in most cases few alternative sources of work existed for skilled employees. They were forced to cooperate in order to maintain their present quality of life.

As the Medieval period progressed, however, the seeds for drastic change were sown. Money replaced land as the principal source of wealth. By the thirteenth century, despite the opposition of the church, the banking industry was well established. The rapid growth of urban centers provided expanding markets. Emphasis shifted slowly from self-sufficiency, a feudal concept based on survival economics, to surplus production, a means of accruing wealth.

MANAGEMENT PRACTICES DURING THE RENAISSANCE

The Italian Renaissance, which began during the fourteenth century, was largely a product of this shift. A hunger for improvement of the individual condition and for self-aggrandizement began to replace the traditional quest for grace and community. It was a period during which craftsmen-owned shops and localism gave way to capitalizer-owned businesses and expansionism. "Capitalism" meant that people began putting their money to work in order to make more money. While technical systems grew more sophisticated during this period, the major change was in the nature of the business social system.

The Renaissance was financed largely by trade with Muslim and Byzantine empires to the east. These connections had been established during the Crusades and were controlled by the city-state of Venice which dominated traffic in the Mediterranean. Countries along the western coast of Europe set sail seeking ocean routes to the East that would allow them to avoid the harsh overland journey and the loss of profits to Venetian and Muslim middlemen. Ships rounded the Cape of Good Hope, establishing trade relations with African, Indian, Japanese, Chinese, and Indonesian cultures. Other adventurers headed west across the Atlantic Ocean in their attempt to discover a shorter route. Instead, they found the North and South American continents.

Despite the tremendous surge of economic growth resulting from cultivation of these new markets and sources of raw materials, the condition of workers in Europe deteriorated. As improvements in technical systems affected both the quality and quantity of goods produced, some guild chapters expanded more rapidly than others, absorbing customers, creating monopolies. The "bourgeoisie" who during the Medieval period had evolved to buy excess goods produced by craftsmen and sell them to different publics for a profit, blossomed into powerful trading and banking families the "fuggers" of Germany, the "merchant princes" of Italy who frequently influenced the decisions of both church and state. Because of this influence, competition could no longer be effectively controlled.

A growing cult of individualism was one of the results of the above-defined change. This cult was tempered in southern Europe by Catholic doctrine which continued to advocate the "family" approach, responsibility to the community, and the belief that grace was more important than profit and personal fame. Farther north, however, in central and northwestern Europe, these constraints were being swept aside.

MANAGEMENT PRACTICES DURING THE REFORMATION

During the Renaissance, craftsmen had begun losing their job security. The Protestant Reformation, which began in the late fifteenth century, unwittingly provided a convenient rationalization for this dilemma. The new religion, which appeared first in Germany, appealed to populations chafing under the restrictions, the heavy taxes, and the corruption of the Catholic Church. It was adopted by individuals interested in gaining greater control over their lives, over the means of improving their earthly status. Martin Luther, the man who initially started and shaped the Reformation, offered this opportunity by abolishing much of the church hierarchy and proclaiming that the priesthood should include all believers, not just those ordained by the church. This proclamation gave the faithful power to make decisions on how to conduct their earthly affairs previously denied.

Another important product of the Reformation espoused by Luther but emphasized by John Calvin, was the doctrine of "salvation by election." This doctrine stated that God alone decided who would be saved and who would be damned. While man was gaining more control over his life on earth, therefore, he had lost at the same time any say in what transpired after death.

Under such a system, as would be expected, focus began shifting away from eternity and toward gaining prosperity in the here and now. Both Luther and Calvin encouraged hard work as a means of improving one's immediate individual situation and benefiting the community. Both, at the same time, warned against exploiting the unfortunate in order to enhance one's personal estate. Economic theory, however, was a relatively unimportant part of this doctrine. The Protestant work ethic, probably the most critical product of the Reformation in terms of our current economic philosophy, was not spelled out in their writings. Rather, it was largely a result of interpretation. As frequently happens, those who took on the task of explaining to the masses what Luther and Calvin had really said and meant tended to stress those parts of the argument most supportive of their own world view.

This emphasis on hard work as a means of turning to profit one's newly awarded control over earthly matters, however, wherever it came from, coupled with the concept of salvation by election, or predestination, strengthened the trend toward individualism. According to some historians, it also encouraged businessmen to ignore Luther's and Calvin's warnings against taking advantage of the unfortunate .

In terms of management philosophy, the "taking care of" part was steadily losing ground. Employees were to be controlled, told what to do, and used to improve one's own earthly situation. Because the employees' fate had been preordained by a higher power, owners did not have to take responsibility for the results of their actions. Profits were the goal. They ensured physical security and a decent life on earth. One of the simplest ways to increase profits was to exploit the efforts of those too weak to resist.

In essence, therefore, the conflict ethic had begun replacing the cooperative ethic in boss/employee relations. "Conflict" occurs when boss/employee "A"'s efforts decrease boss/employee "B"'s chances of fulfilling his or her work related needs/desires and vice versa.

In Europe, small "domestic" shops replaced guild operations and eventually dominated production. Capitalizers brought the raw materials to craftsmen, frequently in their own homes, and picked up the finished pieces. Workers were no longer familiar with markets or marketing procedures. Craftsmen from different towns or different regions might be supplying goods for the same business. These goods might travel across borders or even across oceans to markets. Businesses became networks rather than "families." The element that connected all others was the owner/capitalizer. He alone now understood both production and marketing aspects of the operation. Because he possessed important information that his employees did not have access to, changes in the prices of raw materials and changes in the value of goods on the market, for example, he could improve his own share at their expense.

At the same time, this lack of information prevented employees from contributing meaningfully to management decision-making. Combined with the growing cult of individualism, this change transformed the process into an increasingly individual affair.

The Puritans, Quakers, and Mennonites were Protestant sects persecuted in Europe for their strict adherence to the above philosophy and "strange ways." They emigrated to the New World, settling mainly in what is now the northeastern United States. Thus, they helped define the guiding principles for industrial development in that region and, during one critical period at least, the entire country.

SOCIAL-ECONOMIC THINKING AS THE KEY ISSUE

Before continuing, it is important to consider why the above described evolution in social-economic thinking doctrine occurred. The increasing wealth could easily have been more equitably distributed within the existing system. Much confusion and social conflict could have been avoided by doing so. The societal structures —churches, guilds, governments — required for such distribution were in place. These same institutions had traditionally insured a degree of security, during this life and the next, in return for the support of subjects. Muralists and sculptors, for example, had been taken care of by the church and state while they practiced their art, and helped decorate great cathedrals, palaces, and municipal buildings. Their reward, other than financial, had come from the gratitude of the community served and from glorifying God with their talents. They had been respected, they had been contributing, they had enjoyed the security of being part of a well-defined whole.

Why then, when the opportunity arose, did man immediately begin to strive for individuality? Why did he choose the loneliness of conflict over the security of his previous, cooperative situation? The assurance of God's blessing in return for loyalty was lost. The sense of community with one's fellow man whose purpose was identical, whose level of aspiration was just as limited, also suffered. It was difficult to enjoy communion with someone you were now trying to "beat." Such loneliness is not generally conducive to emotional security. Why, then, were men willing to sacrifice the emotional security offered by the church, their ties with a culture that offered a well-defined purpose, a useful and accepted identity? Why were they not only willing but eager to sacrifice this for an uncertain chance at increased material wealth?

In order to continue our discussion, we must explore more fully the concept of "security." I would break this concept down into two subconcepts -"physical security" and "emotional security."

Physical security relates to things in an individual's environment that influence his or her physical well-being or health. It centers on the search for "enough," on the quest for the inputs necessary to fulfill the individual's basic physical needs. The list includes adequate nutrition and shelter, adequate health care, sufficient educational and employment opportunity, adequate protection from crime, and so on. It is possible to gain physical security without also gaining emotional security.

By emotional security I mean individual achievement of self respect, recognition, and positive self-actualization as relates to the individual's definition of an acceptable purpose in life. Emotional security relates to things in an individual's environment that influence his or her emotional well-being or health. This includes all the factors listed under physical security as well as emotional relationships. Indeed, it is impossible to designate any environmental factor which does not exert some influence on both physical and emotional security. Those unable to develop a reliable source of physical security. Those unable to lift their quality of life above the limit of bare survival, Call rarely enjoy emotional security.

In terms of physical security, then, people of the Medieval period still led an extremely tenuous existence. Hygiene was abominable, especially in the cities. Dysentery was an accepted fact of life. Typhoid and smallpox were rampant. Plague decimated societies periodically, killing approximately one-third of the entire European population during one epidemic alone. People were helpless before these onslaughts. Commoners were also helpless pawns in the power struggles that raged between governments, merchant princes, churches. When armies marched, they lived off the land. Neither citizens nor their belongings were safe in the name of causes that frequently reflected the whims of rulers, rather than the reality of populations.

As long as there seemed no escape from these threats to physical existence, people sought solace in the spiritual life. They were awarded a degree of emotional security by the church in return for obedience and loyalty. This reward centered on the promise of God's forgiveness and a good life in the next world. Commoners were willing to subjugate themselves to the powers that offered this security, to remain nameless, to sacrifice their talents and strength.

But emotional security, as we have said, cannot be complete without physical security. Therefore, once the situation changed and the opportunity appeared to personally enhance one's physical security, to personally make sure one's house was not destroyed next year by invading forces, one's wife was not carried off, one's livestock was not slaughtered, man was willing to fight for it, to risk what he already had in order to obtain it.

Increased wealth seemed to offer such an opportunity. Early profits traditionally had been absorbed by local religion and feudal masters. But no more. As tools and techniques improved, as commerce grew, as the economy expanded, an increasing number of individuals began discovering ways to carve out parcels of their own. With these new riches, men were making sure that they always had enough to eat and a safe place to hide when pestilence or invading armies came. Tomorrow, for them, had become more physically secure, even at the cost of loneliness. They now had a foundation on which to build future physical and emotional security. Others could influence that foundation, but outside forces no longer controlled it.

SUMMARY

In summary then, during the Medieval period guilds dominated production and distribution. The quest was for grace and self sufficiency. Profits were relatively unimportant. All employees participated as decision makers in both the social and technical systems of business. Emphasis was on cooperation. This arrangement resulted from a prevailing "community before the individual socio-economic doctrine, the small size of markets and businesses, the limited nature of competition, and the limited capabilities of current technology.

During the Renaissance the profit motive blossomed and the trading classes began gaining power. As the amount of available wealth grew, increasing numbers of people began renouncing the status quo to seek after it. The church, however, remained powerful and continued to advocate the old virtues. The quest, therefore, was now for grace and profit, rather that for grace and self-sufficiency. Because of "networking," employees no longer had an understanding of business social systems. Their input was limited to their own, small area of technical expertise. Emphasis within the workplace was beginning to swing from cooperation to conflict. Also, markets and businesses were expanding, the number of competitors and the sophistication of technology was increasing.

A new religious doctrine appeared during the Reformation which legitimized and strengthened these trends. It said that profits accrued indicated the individual's chances for gaining grace. The quest, therefore, was now for grace *through* profit rather than for grace *and* profit. Increasing personal wealth became the consuming focus. This doctrine also said that each man was alone in his quest and could not affect the destiny of others. The worker's destiny had already been predetermined. The employer, by exploiting him, was simply fulfilling his own. Social responsibility, therefore, was no longer an issue. Emphasis in the workplace swung sharply toward conflict. Management decision making became an increasingly individual affair.

During the last part of Chapter One I have discussed what I think to be the reasons for the switch from cooperative community efforts to conflict and the quest for individuality. I introduced the concepts of physical and emotional security. Physical security concerns resources necessary to physical survival and well-being. People can have physical security without having emotional security also. Emotional security concerns the achievement of self-respect, recognition, and positive self-actualization In terms of an acceptable purpose in life. People cannot enjoy full emotional security unless they also have physical security.

During the Medieval period few workers could gain physical security, so they accepted the degree of emotional security offered by the church and state. When the chance for physical security materialized during the Renaissance and Reformation periods, however, they were willing to sacrifice their limited amount of emotional security in order to fight for it. This attitude led to radical changes in socio-economic thinking and set the stage for what occurred during the early stages of the Industrial Revolution.

2

The Early Industrial Revolution

TECHNOLOGY AS THE KEY ISSUE

Trends defined in Chapter One gained momentum during the early Industrial Revolution. Prior to the Revolution most craftsmen lived in rural areas and farmed on the side. They were not, therefore, entirely dependent on the money earned from the goods they manufactured for survival. Employers could introduce bonus systems or make threats. They could not, however, truly control employees. The individual craftsman continued to provide his own power and the skills necessary to complete the item manufactured. He decided his daily piece rate. He continued, therefore, to exercise some control over his working life, though he no longer contributed as much to the overall management process.

The Industrial Revolution was generated by radical improvements in key technical systems. It involved a shift from "simple" hand tools to machinery. In England the Revolution was accompanied by and helped make possible simultaneous, radical changes in the agricultural sector. More efficient production techniques such as "enclosure," the consolidation of farms into one continuous land body, were developed. Much "common land," originally open to all for grazing and other uses, was taken over by the powerful. Displaced farm hands drifted from the country to new, urban industrial centers. Once settled in manufacturing cities they lost access to the alternative means of survival available in rural areas. They became completely dependent on factory owners in a culture where socio- economic thinking not only accepted exploitation, but encouraged it.

The role of the employee in the manufacturing process also changed with this shift. Workers no longer produced salable goods directly, providing their own power and skill. They now operated machines powered by outside sources of energy which produced goods, or parts of goods. Their level of participation had again been diminished.

THE THEORETICAL RATIONALIZATION

The Early Industrial Revolution Era rationale for this frequently exclusive quest for increased physical security was the doctrine generated by the classical economists. These men taught that the greatest good for the greatest number would be achieved by allowing individuals to pursue their own, enlightened self-interest. Though this was economic rather that religious reasoning, its roots obviously still fed off the Reformation. The lure and increasingly obvious benefits of materialistic wealth had blinded many to the dangers of such a self-centered and lopsided approach to improvement of the human condition. Important advocates of this rationale were the Scottish philosopher Adam Smith, whose popular doctrine of "'laissez-faire'' economics appeared in his 1776

book entitled *The Wealth of Nations,* and Thomas Malthus, an Anglican clergyman, whose theory on population growth was published in his 1798 "Essay on Population."
Smith said that the world of economics had its own natural laws, much like the physical world. Supply and demand was the most basic of these laws. Competition, in conjunction with the amount of goods available and market fluctuations, would keep the economy in balance if the process was unimpeded by government intervention.

Malthus's work excused the inhumane treatment of workers. He said that because population increased geometrically while the food supply increased only by arithmetic ratio, eventually we would not have enough to feed everyone. Famine and strife would follow. This pronouncement was interpreted to mean that because the working class produced most of the world's children, betterment of its situation would only cause a population explosion which, in turn, would bring everyone to grief. Employers were doing society a favor by keeping workers impoverished.

The workplace was being rapidly dehumanized. Emphasis was now entirely on efficiency, no matter what the human cost. Laborers had fallen victim to "mechanical authoritarianism." They no longer controlled what they did. Rather, they now had to meet the demands of machines to which they were sometimes physically chained.

Even in instances where machines had not been installed, production had been broken down into efficiency-increasing steps. Each worker repeated one stage in the process continually, instead of manufacturing a completed item. Adam Smith estimated that such an arrangement in a pin factory allowed workers to increase their productivity by 240 times. He also noted, however, that such labor "tended to make human beings as stupid and ignorant as it is possible for a human being to become."[1]

INITIAL EFFECTS ON MANAGEMENT PROCESSES

During the early stages of the Industrial Revolution, then, efforts were made to transform the social system at the production level into part of the technical system. Only managers and machines existed. Some of the machines were human beings. Their human strengths, weaknesses, and needs, however, were largely ignored. Standards used to evaluate employee performance were the same used to evaluate machine performance. Machines, by definition, at this point in history at least, could not "think." Production level workers functioned as machine parts and, therefore, could not think either. They had no contribution to make to the decision making process.

This approach succeeded for several reasons. First, businesses were still of a controllable size. Top management could make all important decisions without slowing the production process unacceptably. Second, technology was still relatively simple and was evolving at a pace that allowed management to maintain the necessary level of understanding. Third, through free enterprise a relatively small number of individuals had been able to gain control of key resources and markets, restrict competition, and run the economy to their own advantage. Fourth, those in control were strong enough to force decisions on government and consumers even if such decisions were not in the public's best interest. When they made mistakes, the cost was not crippling. Required raw materials were cheap and often seemingly inexhaustible. An excess of labor existed. If employees were driven to rebellion by unacceptable working conditions, they could be dealt with summarily and replaced. Fifth, the age of the individual had reached its zenith. The Horatio Alger type hero was in vogue. "Self-made men," those who had gained the greatest shares of physical security, were respected by the multitude, no matter what the cost of their accomplishments to themselves, their families, their communities, or their environment. This was the age of industrial giants. In the United States, where the era was most flamboyant, we had individuals like Jay Gould, Jim Fisk, J. P. Morgan, Philip Armour, Andrew Carnegie, James Hill, John Rockefeller, Collis Huntington, Leland Stanford, and Jay Cook.

The above ' heroes" or "robber barons," depending on your point of view, who gained control of and ordered an unparalleled period of economic growth, were mainly austere men driven by ambition, frequently to the point of ruthlessness. Most of them had grown up in strict, Protestant, New England poverty. Their Reformation-spawned socio-economic thinking designated idleness and extravagance as cardinal sins. Their major reward in life was the acquisition of wealth and power. They built monuments to themselves, but rarely pursued pleasure for its own sake. Time spent in the pursuit of anything other than profit was considered wasted.

As the Revolution progressed, the form of businesses changed rapidly. Individual proprietors and partnerships were replaced by chartered corporations. This arrangement insured the relative permanence of organizations, limited liability for stockholders, and provided adequate capital for promoters. It also allowed the organization of financial structures upon which monopolies could be based. Three distinct employee layers appeared in the typical business hierarchy—the capitalist-controller, middle management in charge of production, and the workers. The layers were segregated. The capitalist-controller planned the organization's future and controlled finances. Middle management made sure production quotas were met. Laborers did what they were told. The segregation existed not only in terms of responsibility; it was also physical. Controllers were usually far removed from work sites. They spent their time in the financial and political capitals, battling to expand their empires. Most managers spent little time on the shop floor. Problems were sent up, solutions were sent down.

The Industrial Revolution, however, while it initially allowed the chosen few to accumulate more physical security, fame, and power than ever before possible, eventually contributed to the demise of such ascendancy. At the same time, it made individual domination of the management decision making process no longer practical. It created the need for labor to once again contribute.

ONGOING CHANGES IN BUSINESS SOCIAL SYSTEMS THAT AFFECTED THE MANAGEMENT PROCESS

In terms of social systems, workers were beginning to question the rationalization that their plight had been predestined. They were also beginning to overcome their dependence on others for relief. The realization that they could both individually and as a group influence present and future circumstances grew rapidly. The major means of doing this was by organizing. The networking system of cottage industries had kept workers from communicating. The factory system brought them together. Factory owners packed employees in to witness each other's fate, to share grievances, to begin defining their power as a class. They glimpsed the physical security gained by others from their efforts and wanted more for themselves.

The organization of labor began in England during the eighteenth century when skilled artisans in different trades banded together to protect their wage standards which were being battered by competition. Parliament responded to pleas for help by making such organizations illegal and forcing them underground. Harsh penalties, including death, were meted out to workers who conspired together maliciously "to injure their masters and employers by quitting their work on account of their demands for an increase in wages not being acceded to."[2]

The working class, however, found champions. Opposition to the theories of Adam Smith, Malthus, and others supporting exploitation grew. While the above classical economists called themselves "liberals," a second group of "liberals" materialized whose thoughts were more like those of their modern day counterparts.

Possibly the best known of this latter group was John Stuart Mill. While Mill supported the free enterprise system, he argued in his 1848 book, *Principles* of *Political Economics,* that the state must provide physical security for the poor. He believed that the law of supply and demand should regulate production, but not distribution. The state, for example, should offer free education to all. Money for such efforts should be raised through income and inheritance taxes. Others in this group were more radical, but all called for increased regulation by the state and a fairer, forced distribution of the wealth.

By the early 1820's unions were tolerated in England. Movements for universal male suffrage, however, the key to total legalization, failed until 1867. Then, with unions rapidly gaining strength, a Reform Bill was passed which allowed the industrial proletariat to vote. By 1875 all anti-union laws had been repealed.

The legalization and coming to power of unions in France and Germany occurred at roughly the same time. Organizations representing labor formed in France as part of the 1792 Revolution. These, however, were soon outlawed. Continuing unionization efforts were sometimes supported, sometimes brutally suppressed by a series of relatively unstable governments. It was not until the rise of the Third Republic following the tragedy of the Commune when hundreds of protesting and rioting workers were shot by troops that uninterrupted growth began. Official recognition was received in 1884.

In Germany attempts to organize workers were initiated by socialist elements in the late 1840's As part of preparations for the Franco-Prussian War unions were legalized in 1869. Following that war, however, the government, led by Bismarck, used anti-socialist laws to quash the movement. German courts upheld the right of unions to exist in 1882, as long as they stayed out of politics. In 1890 expiration of the socialist laws freed unions from 311 legal constraints.

In the United States the Industrial Revolution started later than in the more economically advanced European countries. Trade unions began forming between 1861 and 1866. The first group to attract a serious following was the Knights of Labor, a secret society formed in 1869. The Knights began organizing unskilled labor. Their eventual demands included: I) an eight hour day; 2) arbitration in industrial disputes; 3) equal pay for equal work for both sexes; 4) prohibition of child labor; 5) establishment of a bureau of labor statistics; 6) enactment of safety and health codes; 7) laws compelling employers to pay workers weekly; 8) recognition of the incorporation of labor unions; 9) prohibition of contract foreign labor; 10) abolition of national banks; 11) imposition of an income tax; 12) government ownership of railroads and telegraph lines.

A majority of these demands related to gaining greater physical security-increased pay, safer working conditions, less competition for existing jobs. Very few, if any, of the demands were directly concerned with gaining greater emotional security. The attention of most workers, at this point in history, remained on development of an adequate physical "foundation."

The unionization movement in the United States was fiercely opposed by the robber barons who considered labor simply another challenger to defeat in their quest for the power which was their due according to endowment, upbringing, and effort. The barons manipulated the government and courts in their efforts to win. The battle was fierce. Between 1880 and 1900 a yearly average of 1,190 strikes affecting 330,500 workers in 6,372 businesses occurred.[3] By the turn of the century, however, labor was making steady if erratic progress. World War I found management and unions sitting down together with government to plan the war economy. Labor, by this time, had become a major economic and political force.

ONGOING CHANGES IN BUSINESS TECHNICAL SYSTEMS THAT AFFECTED THE MANAGEMENT PROCESS

From the middle of the seventeenth to the middle of the eighteenth century desire on the part of German guilds to protect their power slowed technological development in that country. In France, the unstable nature of a series of governments hampered development. England, however, was different. Guilds there began to lose their power relatively early. Innovators could proceed pretty much as they pleased.

Also, the approach to technological development in continental Europe was largely rationalistic, theory-oriented. French scientists wanted to know why a system behaved the way it did. The British, on the other hand, were more empirical, application-oriented. They were chiefly interested in discovering how many uses a new technology could be put to. This emprirical mind-set, coupled with the government's laissez-faire attitude, allowed the British to progress more rapidly in the organization of production. The concurrence of Watt's invention of the steam engine in 1769 with improvements in the smelting process of iron made large scale machinery possible. The next quarter century produced a parade of related developments. These included the steam locomotive, the machine tool industry that facilitated mass production systems, a mechanical loom which revolutionized the fabric industry, and innovations in the science and technology of electricity. Britain led the way and profited most from these results. By the last quarter of the century Britain was producing more industrial goods than the rest of the world combined.

Due partially, however, to its lack of support for popular education, Britain's lead was lost soon thereafter. Scientific and technological development in England had traditionally been carried on by individuals. The current, rapid growth of international competition, however, made this approach inefficient. The German government had long since begun funding technological institutes and laboratories. In the United States similar facilities were being financed partially by the state, partially by industrialists. Enormous sums had been contributed by the latter. As Alfred Whitehead, the British mathematician and philosopher, wrote, " the greatest invention of the nineteenth century was the invention of the method of inventions."[4] By "method of inventions" he referred to the new institutions that provided scientific and other academic resources for the solution of industrial problems.

THE INVOLVEMENT OF ACADEMIA

The above defined movement precipitated a major shift for academia. Traditionally, colleges and universities had remained aloof from the pragmatic, results-oriented, materialistic world of industry. Now they were becoming rapidly involved. In the United States, Rensselaer Polytechnic Institute was founded in 1824. It was followed by the Rochester Institute of Technology in 1829, the Massachusetts Institute of Technology in 1861, the Worcester Polytechnical Institute in 1865, the Stevens Institute of Technology in 1867, the Virginia Polytechnical Institute in 1872, the Michigan Technological Institute in 1885, and many other institutions built to deal specifically with technical systems issues.

Academia's first recognized effort to deal with industry's social system problems began later, in 1881, when Joseph Wharton gave the University of Pennsylvania $100,000 to start a management department. By 1911, 30 such departments were in operation. Because employees were still viewed as extensions of the machines operated, early theoreticians talked mainly in terms of increased efficiency.

The more closely social systems resembled their technical counterparts, the more efficient they would be. Perhaps the best known spokesman for this "mechanistic" approach was the engineer Frederick Taylor. Previously defined management practices had been based largely on experience and/or instinct. Taylor introduced scientific method. His approach, called "Scientific Management," was not entirely new. Plato had discussed its key principle, the division of labor, in his book *The Republic*. Only with the advent of the factory system, however, did scientific management achieve its true potential. Sir James Stueart in his 1767 book, An *Inquiry into the Principles of Political Economy*, was the first to explore its possible applications in depth. The Soho Foundry of Great Britain, started in 1800 to manufacture Watt's steam engine, utilized a broad range of "Scientific Management" concepts including market research, work flow analysis, and cost accounting.

Taylor, whose main contributions occurred during the late 1880's and early 1900's, was best remembered for his emphasis on "time studies." His technique involved finding the "one best way" to perform every operation in a manufacturing process. After this "one best way" had been discovered, it was timed with a stopwatch. Workers were then trained and quotas set according to the findings. Monetary incentives were established to encourage the achievement and surpassing of quotas. A major requirement for the success of this system, according to Taylor, was that employees should be "extremely stupid." They should not be allowed to think. They should only listen and do what they were told. "The time during which man stops to think is part of the time that he is not productive . "[5]

Other contributors to the school of scientific management included Frank Gilbreth who introduced "motion studies," a means of increasing worker productivity through the analysis of job-related movements; Henry Gantt who developed the "Gantt Chart," a daily balance sheet which plotted output against task time; Harrington Emerson, an "efficiency engineer" who emphasized standardization; and Henry Tayol, a Frenchman ahead of his time who developed the first comprehensive theory of management. Another key figure was Hugo Munsterberg, a psychologist and forerunner of the next important evolutionary stage in management theory. By 1910 he had begun research dealing with the application of psychology to industry.

These men were interested mainly in improving productivity through regimentation, manipulation, and incentives. Their focus was on managerial problems. They had not yet taken into account labor's viewpoint. None of them had progressed far enough in their research to seriously address the potential contribution of workers beyond their defined roles in the production process. The traditional hierarchy and lines of authority/responsibility stood unassailed. Decision making remained strictly the province of managers and executives.

As we see, therefore, the conflict ethic remained dominant. The individual reigned supreme. As the Revolution progressed, however, it became increasingly obvious that change was necessary if industry was to remain healthy. My task in Chapter Three is to discuss the beginnings of such change.

SUMMARY

In summary then, modifications that greatly affected the nature of problem solving occurred in business social and technical systems during the early Industrial Revolution. Originally, emphasis was on making the social system part of the technical system. One difference between man and machine, however, could not be negated. Whereas machines were given their purpose and could not deviate without external intervention, man was capable of defining and changing his. The ability of workers to appraise their environment, to compare their situation with that of peers, management, and owner-controllers could not be turned off. The social system remained, therefore, very much alive.

After an initial period of helplessness and adjustment, workers began identifying objectives and the means of achieving them. The major goal, at that point, was increased physical security, a greater share of the profits generated. While workers no longer helped make decisions concerning the production of wealth, they demanded an increasing voice in the question of its distribution.

The way to gain such a voice was to organize. By forming unions and acting in concert, workers could strongly affect the success of business operations. They could also become a potent political force and push for expanded educational opportunity. By gaining education they could better understand relevant processes and improve their individual wealth generating abilities. Workers fought for the right to unionize. Unions, in turn, with support from humanists, fought for a political voice and a more open education system.

During the early Industrial Revolution, however, tremendous resistance also existed to rapid improvement of the worker's situation. The legalization of unions was a slow and often brutal process. Governments were traditionally a bastion of the economically powerful. Politics reflected the needs and desires of a small elite, rather than of the general population. Workers and their supporters had to struggle for the right to vote. They had to overcome the monarchists belief that education of the masses was dangerous, rather than advantageous, to industrial society. The highest levels of the educational ladder were denied commoners in Europe until the twentieth century.

In the late 1800's and early 1900's academia became involved in the solution of industry's technical and, later, socio-system management problems. Initially its perspective was that of management. Researchers focused mainly on enhancing the "mechanical" efficiency of workers. They had not yet explored labor's viewpoint and addressed issues such as the potential value of worker participation in the decision making process. As the environment grew increasingly complex, however, both academia and management realized that labor had to play a greater role if industry was to thrive. Attempts to define the nature of this new role are the subject of Chapter Three.

NOTES

1. David Jenkins, *Job Power* (Baltimore: Penguin Books, 1973), p. 23.

2. Walter Galenson, ed., *Comparative Labor Movements* (New York: Russell & Russell, 1952), p. 3.

3. John Krout, *United: States Since 1865* (New York: Barnes and Noble, 1955), p. 59.

4. D. S. L. Cardwell, *Turning Points in Western Technology* (New York: Neale Watson Academic Publications, 1972), p. 261.

5. Jenkins, p. 28.

3

The Middle Era

MANAGEMENT'S DILEMMA

Changes in the management processes of western business communities came from two directions as the Industrial Revolution progressed. The first was bottom-up. Workers began to demand a larger say in the distribution of the wealth produced and a greater share of the control over their work environment.

The second direction was top-down. Management gradually realized that if the most efficient solutions were to be achieved, employees had to be involved. This realization, however, carried with it a need for changes that directly repudiated prevailing socio-economic doctrine. That doctrine continued to be based on the protestations of Luther and Calvin. It was supported by the eighteenth century works of Smith and Malthus and by the nineteenth century research of the biological scientist, Charles Darwin. In an 1859 book entitled *The Origin of the Species,* Darwin presented his theory of "natural selection." He attempted to prove that different species of life on earth evolved and improved because of a natural process by which only the strongest specimens, the most adaptable, survived. Herbert Spencer in Britain and William Graham Sumner in the United States led efforts to relate these findings to human society. They and their followers were called Social Darwinists. Spencer and Sumner described social phenomena in terms of conflict. The essence of their philosophy was "every man for himself," "survival of the fittest." Man was part of God's nature. It was wrong, therefore, for him to tamper with nature's laws, as defined by Darwin, and try to prevent the strong from taking advantage of the weak.

Many industrialists on both sides of the ocean grasped this revelation as a further excuse for their self-centered pursuit of physical security, their lack of concern for the plight of workers. Nature, now, as well as God, was offering justification for their excesses.

Management was, at this point, trapped in a dilemma. On one side lay centuries of relatively comfortable tradition. On the other lurked the extremely pragmatic realization that if decision making systems were not improved, production systems might become less efficient Initially, at least, tradition held sway. The vast majority of management teams opted for the status quo. As a result of this consensus the unsatisfactory consequences of their decision could be and usually were attributed to the wrong factor or factors. Because an insignificant number of companies chose to modify their problem solving process, no revealing comparisons could be made.

THE HUMAN RELATIONS MOVEMENT

Most changes in management practices during the middle part of the Industrial Revolution, therefore, occurred initially because of "bottom-up" pressures. Social scientists, in their continuing quest for a more useful definition of the "problematique," had become increasingly interested in labor's viewpoint. In order to make workers more productive it was now considered necessary to understand their feelings, their needs and desires. During the 1920's and 1930's the "Human Relations" school evolved in reaction to Taylor's "Scientific Management." A notable forerunner of this school was the Englishman, Oliver Sheldon, who, in his 1923 book, *The Philosophy of Management,* declared that the key problem of industry was to determine the proper balance between the "things of production" and the "humanity of production." He viewed industry as "a body of men" rather than a "mass of machines and technical processes." Sheldon proposed that the following rules be followed in respect to all employees:[1] 1) they should help design their working environment; 2) they should receive means for achieving a respectable standard of living. 3) they should have adequate leisure time for self development; 4) they should be secure from involuntary unemployment; 5) they should share profits according to their contribution; and 6) a strict spirit of equality should be found in management-labor relations. Sheldon, as we see, was beginning to talk about emotional as well as physical security.

Two other key figures in this school were the American, Mary Follet, and the Australian, Elton Mayo. Follet said that man on the job was motivated by the same needs and desires which motivated him otherwise. One of these was the need for a degree of control over his situation. She believed that coordination, rather than intimidation, was the essence of good management. While at Harvard, Mayo conducted an extensive series of experiments and studies to support his hypothesis that "logical factors were far less important than emotional factors in determining productive efficiency." He studied employee cultures, espousing the value of "group endeavors' to achieve cooperatively defined objectives. Emphasis had begun shifting, then, from mechanistic, efficiency improving studies to identification of employee needs and desires. In general, practitioners believed that by improving employee "on the job" social satisfaction they could also increase productivity. One of the techniques that eventually evolved from this movement in the United States was "job enlargement." This technique was developed at the University of Michigan's Institute for Social Research and involved the enhancement of jobs with additional, related tasks. The worker could rotate between these tasks as a means of combatting boredom and of developing a sense of personal competence and responsibility. In general, the objective of those advocating "job enrichment" was to make work more meaningful. Another, later result of this movement was the technique of "job enrichment," the development of which was attributed largely to Frederick Herzberg of Columbia University. "Job enrichment" included workers in planning and control activities as well. It, therefore, stimulated and enriched interaction between hierarchical levels and between peers on the same level.

The major weakness of these approaches, however, became rapidly apparent. Workers were still being manipulated. Instead of being programmed simply to produce more, they were now being programmed to enjoy producing more. Possibly as a result of this weakness, follow-up studies showed that productivity sometimes increased, sometimes decreased in the aftermath of such exercises, or that productivity increased initially because of the additional attention paid subjects, then tapered off again when the project ended.

The major contribution of the human relations school, in

retrospect, was its redefinition of labor. Workers were now more frequently viewed as human beings with needs and desires differing from those of machines. Failure to treat employees as such came to be regarded as a cause of low morale, sloppiness, antagonism, and, eventually, lack of productivity. Progressive management, with the support of unions, redeveloped a conscience. It became patronizing. Companies reverted to the "control and take care of" philosophy found during the Medieval period.

ORGANIZATIONAL SIZE/DESIGN AS THE KEY ISSUE

Meanwhile, businesses continued to grow in size as a result of the expansion of markets and mergers. As with guilds during the Renaissance period, companies better able to interpret and take advantage of changes in their environment swallowed those less capable of doing so. This increase in size exacerbated the inefficiency of the decision making apparatus for the following reasons.

The first had to do with organization design. Businesses were structured as hierarchical bureaucracies. This arrangement had traditionally served two purposes. First, according to Daniel Katz and Robert Kahn in their book *The Social Psychology of Organizations*, it allowed organizations to reduce "the variability, instability and spontaneity" of employee behavior to a manageable level.[2] Second, the hierarchical bureaucracy was thought to enhance decision making efficiency by streamlining the movement of information. This same structure, however, was also eventually identified as a deterrent to such efficiency. A "bureaucracy," as defined by Max Weber, the German philosopher, was a "rigid and stable body of rules, sanctions and offices which governed the entire organization. Responsibility was specifically assigned to certain officials and duties were carried out according to fixed regulation. The organization of offices followed the principle of hierarchy."³ Emphasis centered on uniformity and precision. Roles, lines of authority, and responsibilities were clearly defined. Although this arrangement initially reduced confusion, as organizations grew it also bred new obstacles.

One of these obstacles was the bureaucracy's tendency to encourage a mechanistic process. Limited roles with limited responsibility were predefined. People were fitted into these roles with little concern for other abilities they might possess. Resources allocated for the development of employee potential were scarce or nonexistent. Bureaucrats, therefore, even if they wanted to, were largely incapable of utilizing advantageously the potential of a majority of their employees.

A second obstacle resulted from the fact that the hierarchical structure of bureaucracies reinforced the cult of "individualism." Bosses were designated and given symbols of rank and authority such as an individual office, an office with a window, a secretary, and so forth. This system reinforced the conflict ethic. The boss's mission was frequently to utilize the talents of subordinates as fully as possible without allowing them to appear too good. The subordinate's mission was to impress the boss with a performance superior to that of peers without threatening him. Much energy was wasted "politicking," defending one's status, worrying about or attacking the competition. Such an atmosphere was not conducive to truly efficient management.

A third obstacle resulted from the tendency of large bureaucracies to stifle the flow of information. The hierarchical arrangement formalized the separation of management decision makers from the workers who implemented those decisions. In some U.S. companies as many as 14 or 15 layers of personnel existed in the chain of command. Questions, concerns, and responses had to travel through the levels and were often modified according to various perspectives so that the initiator received inappropriate feedback. Also, hierarchical etiquette slowed the flow of information, which in turn slowed other corporate processes.

A fourth obstacle resulted from the fact that hierarchies discourage innovation. Because one had limited contact with those above and was not sure of how they would react, the tendency was to play it safe. In some instances top management might say it wanted new ideas, even offer incentives. The potential innovator then had to worry about in-between bosses whose approval was necessary and who might be threatened by the aggressive behavior of subordinates.

A fifth obstacle resulted from the fact that bureaucracy staff units traditionally had no bottom line responsibility. Their efficiency could not be questioned directly. Their value could not be measured in terms of profits. Size, the number of people controlled, became a criterion for success. Such growth, however, had to be justified by increased output. Staff units, therefore, began creating work. They became overly involved in the decision making process, creating red tape and unnecessary bottlenecks.

The second reason that rapid growth of business size exacerbated the inefficiency of the decision making apparatus had to do with environment. Due partially to the inherent inflexibility of bureaucracies, due partially to the size of investments required for technology and equipment modification, large businesses were unable to adapt to the increasing rate of environmental change, to meet the growing demands of both customers and government regulation. Instead of seeking ways to deal adequately with such turbulence, many companies adopted a reactive or inactive stance. Resources were wasted on ultimately futile attempts to arrest change. Thus companies which polluted, for example, spent a great deal of money lobbying against stricter environmental standards, scapegoating the government for lagging profits, avoiding the real issues.

THE FORMATION OF WORKER COUNCILS

In an era when speed and accuracy of input were rapidly becoming more important, management, academia, and, to a lesser extent, labor, whose attention still centered on increasing physical security, realized the need to overcome the constraints of tradition and size and to develop internal systems that allowed businesses to learn from their environments and adapt. Drastic reform was impossible for several reasons. First, no one was sure what the exact nature of such reform should be. Too many people stood to lose too much if a mistake was made. Second, the means of convincing stakeholders emotionally, if not logically, of the need for such reform were not readily available. The situation had not yet become threatening enough.

The first limited step taken involved the expansion of previous efforts to improve interlevel communication. Between the end of World War II and 1950 "Worker Councils" materialized in the industrial society of at least five Western European countries—Norway, France, Sweden, Holland, and Germany. These councils were joint labor-management committees formed to discuss both technical and social issues at the corporate level. Their value was that they brought labor and management into still closer personal contact.

They also gave labor the opportunity to develop a more wholistic perspective of the company's operations. A third value, from management's viewpoint, was that decisions could be reached more quickly. When management required labor's support, it could present selected facts directly and deal with repercussions immediately, instead of going through channels. Management decision making, therefore, became more efficient in terms of speed, if not content.

The Councils' chief weakness was their solely advisory nature. Most had no decision making power. A second weakness was their lack of access to relevant information. This lack placed council members, especially worker representatives, at a disadvantage when discussing issues or suggesting modifications. Management listened, but retained firm control of the process. It could continue to manipulate labor under the guise of cooperation. A third weakness was labor's inability to adequately address many of the issues presented. I frequently council representatives had not received the technical training necessary. A fourth weakness was that, because of their ineffectiveness, labor's representatives frequently lost the confidence and, therefore, the support and input of fellow employees.

THE TAVISTOCK ALTERNATIVE

An alternative or complementary approach to increased participation in problem solving was developed and advocated by the Tavistock Institute of England. This approach did not include lower level employees in the consideration of corporate level issues. Rather, it involved them in the solution of problems faced in their daily assignment, problems which affected them directly. Such problems generally concerned job design and the work environment.

43

A 1950's project completed by Eric Trist of Tavistock and his associates for the recently nationalized British coal industry illustrates actualization of this approach. Traditionally the organization of labor in the mines had been based on principles of scientific management. The task of removing a "face" of coal had been broken down into simple steps. Each member of the work team had been a "specialist" who performed one step continuously, be it digging the coal out, advancing tunnel roof supports, or loading the coal for removal. Pay rates had been defined for each of these positions with individual incentives based on productivity.

Trist turned these teams into autonomous work groups. After being given an assignment, the group members themselves were allowed to decide how to accomplish it. They were allowed to decide who would do which task and for how long. They were responsible for training members to new tasks. Individual pay was based on group performance. As a result of these changes, productivity increased drastically, absenteeism declined.

Possibly the most unique and revolutionary feature of the Tavistock approach was the complete relinquishment of responsibility and authority concerning the solution of production problems to the employees who did the producing. A second important feature, related to the first, was the concept of "holism". Members, it was found, were more efficient when combining their skills to address a "complete" task than when forced to focus on a segregated, individual component of that task.

The autonomous work group approach was then adopted and experimented with by other western industrial powers. Several major Swedish corporations, for example, have attempted to institute versions of it. The Volvo case is perhaps the best known. Plant production personnel were organized into groups of "specialists" and assigned "zones" over which they exercised complete control. The various specialist groups could subdivide into as many work teams as they desired and assemble as many left front car doors, for example, at a time as they wished. The groups were responsible for their own quality control. Their only contract with management was to deliver a specified number of finished components each day.

LIKERT'S HOLISTIC APPROACH

In the United States, during this same period, the work of Rensis Likert, part of the University of Michigan group, was generating interest. Likert focused on developing a more "holistic" approach to improving the quality of working life overall. He realized the need for all employees to understand their corporation's mission and their individual role in achieving it. He realized also that corporations must understand and help employees reach personal objectives. Likert said that the best way to implement and sustain such two-way support was through the participation of all stakeholders in the problem solving process at all levels, the lowest as well as the highest. Likert's major contribution was his realization that a new organizational design was needed to facilitate such overall participation. Organizational charts should show, rather that building blocks forming a pyramid, a series of overlapping circles. The circles represented work groups, each with a specific mission. The overlapping areas represented "link-pin" individuals who belonged to more than one group and, therefore, facilitated communication. This, we could say, was Tavistock's autonomous work groups concept applied to the organization as a whole.

ROADBLOCKS TO CHANGE

Despite their importance, however, contributions of the above mentioned scientists and their colleagues eventually aroused more interest in academic than in management circles. Although the work of the Tavistock Institute staff and other researchers provided a breakthrough in terms of increasing productivity, the lessons learned were usually ignored. The implications for management were too threatening. Although a growing body of evidence supported the belief that properly designed participative decision making was more efficient, at least on production levels of the hierarchy, large scale change did not occur.

One specific roadblock was middle management. Middle management's major responsibility had traditionally been control of the daily routine including short-term problem solving on the operational level. Early efforts to improve the problem solving process had focused on increasing worker participation. If labor proved itself capable of addressing short-term operational problems just as efficiently or even more efficiently than their bosses, middle management would lose its most important role.

Thus, middle managers were trapped in a no-win pincer movement. Participation-minded labor and its supporters were pushing bottom-up. Efficiency-minded executives were pushing top-down. As might be expected, morale began to drop. In a 1973 survey of nearly 3,000 executives conducted by the American Management Association almost one-half of the middle managers queried said their jobs were "at best unsatisfactory."[4] An ongoing poll conducted by the Opinion Research Corporation has asked three work force sectors middle management, hourly workers, and clerical workers to rate their work situation in terms of the following eleven issues.

1) How would you rate this company as a place to work compared with other companies or organizations you know or have heard about?

2) How do you like your job the kind of work you do?

3) Overall, how would you rate the department in which you work?

4) Rating of company on treating you with respect as an individual.

5) Rating of company on willingness to listen to your problems and complaints.

6) Rating of company on doing something about your problems and complaints.

7) Rating of company on letting you know what is going on in the company.

8) When the company gives out information to employees, how do you feel about it?

9) Rating of company on providing job security.

10) Rating of company on opportunity for advancement.

11) Rating of company on your pay.

Concerning all issues, the percentage of positive responses from middle management dropped off, sometimes precipitously after 1977. At the same time the percentage of positive

responses from hourly workers climbed after 1977 in all but four cases (1), (2), (6), (11) and the percentage of positive responses from clerical workers climbed in all but five (I), (2), (4), (8). (11).5
While the gap between labor and middle management seemed to be narrowing dangerously, that between middle management and upper level management was perceived as growing. It appeared that corporate executives were sacrificing middle management in order to maintain their own integrity as individual decision makers. Middle management should encourage the involvement of labor in the solution of production problems. At the same time, however, middle management was not qualified to assist directly in the solution of strategic issues.

This, although alternative approaches to problem solving began to metalized during the Middle Era, they were not generally accepted. Worker participation went against tradition. It contradicted lingering socio-economic doctrine and the related conflict ethic. It disrupted hierarchically defined and bureaucratically enforced lines of responsibility and authority. Eventually, most stakeholders realized that still more basic changes had to occur in key environmental variables if the required adjustments were to become acceptable. How these changes were defined will be the subject of Chapter Four.

SUMMARY

In summary, a new management paradigm began to emerge in western industrial society during the Middle Era. It was the result of a continuing redefinition of the relationship between socio and technical systems in the workplace. This redefinition originated during the early Industrial Revolution as a reaction to scientific management and other dehumanizing trends. Its evolution was stimulated by labor's desire for a greater share of the physical security generated, as well as by management's realization that total domination of the problem solving process was no longer efficient.

Desirable change, however, as defined by the "Human Relations" school, was impeded by business size and tradition. Those in power clung to the old organizational system, to the hierarchical bureaucracy. While progressive upper level managers conceded that such change might be beneficial on lower levels, they did not want it to affect their own. Middle management, in turn, balked at sharing its principal responsibility, the solution of production related problems. And finally, labor remained chiefly interested in gaining a larger share of the available physical security. It showed at this point little concern for flagging operational efficiency.

As is frequently the case with social evolution, real change began occurring only when a true crisis materialized. The nature of this crisis and its effects on the problem solving process are the subject of Chapter Four.

NOTES

1. Claude George, *The History of Management Thought* (Englewood Cliffs, N.J.: Prentice-Hall, 1968), pp. 125-28.

2. Daniel Katz and Robert Kahn, *The Social Psychology of Organizations* (New York: Wiley, 1967), p. 99.

3. David Jenkins, *Job Power* (Baltimore: Penguin Books, 1974), p. 32.

4. Thomas J. Murray, "The Revolt of the Middle Manager Phase Two," *Dun's*, August 1973, p. 32.

5. Michael Cooper, Peter Gelfond, and Patricia Foley, "Early Warning Signals Growing Discontent Among Managers," *Business*, January-February 1980, pp. 3-10.

4

The Late
Industrial Revolution

MARKETPLACE PRESSURE
AS THE KEY ISSUE

In retrospect, advocates of participative management realized that neither the strictly top-down nor the strictly bottom-up approach worked. As Likert had said, a more holistic perspective was required, one that took into account the needs of all employee levels simultaneously. The importance of this realization was intensified by the fact that a crisis had materialized. The crisis resulted not so much from contradictions in the western management paradigm as it did from the increasing growth and efficiency of foreign competitors.

The Industrial Revolution gained impetus more slowly in the rest of the world than it did in Western Europe and the United States. Following World War II, however, many "underdeveloped" countries expanded their production capability rapidly. Most of them enjoyed two key advantages: 1) Because of an initial dependence on western sources for financing and technological expertise, they were able to study the history of western industrial development, to define efficiency-limiting mistakes and to search for alternative approaches; and 2) the Asian cultures, especially, enjoyed a more adaptable socio-economic doctrine. In western industrial society, the conflict ethic still dominated. Conflict involves win-lose situations. One party necessarily gains at the other's expense. Conflict, as defined in Chapter One, existed in the internal environment between labor and management over the distribution of profits. Conflict existed in the transactional environment between companies over raw material supplies and market shares. Conflict existed in the contextual environment between the corporate world and government over excess regulation, consumer protection, and environmental protection issues.

In the most advanced Asian industrial power, Japan, which we shall use as an example, different relationships evolved between the above defined stakeholders groups. A cooperative ethic, (as defined in Chapter One,) was cultivated in the internal environment. Emphasis was on creating a Win-Win situation. This emphasis resulted from a variety of cultural factors. One was religion. The Shinto tradition and Karm encouraged racial pride and nationalism. Confucianism was a moral code based on the interlocking social obligation of practitioners. According to Zen Buddhism one achieved the blessed state of Nirvana by leading a selfless and harmonious life. Another factor was the paternalistic nature of the society. Corporations became extensions of the primary family.

A less positive motivation, however, was the fact that an adequate welfare net did not fully materialize in Japan until 1973 when the social security system was restructured. Also, many of the Japanese system's employee benefits now lauded by other cultures were largely the product of union pressures mounted after World War II.

The role of Japanese unions, however, changed more rapidly than that of their western counterparts. Currently the Japanese union's main purpose is to express the solidarity of labor in disagreements with management. Short strikes are generally demonstrations of this solidarity, rather than attempts to force management concessions by hampering the organization's ability to produce.

Corporate problem solving is frequently accomplished by a team of management and labor representatives in Japan. No decisions are finalized without total agreement. Such an approach, though facilitating implementation, obviously lengthens the decision making process. This shortcoming, however, is made less of a constraint by the absence of time-consuming adversarial interaction. The approach, therefore, is relatively efficient in terms of both time expended and the reliability of solutions.

A competitive ethic was cultivated between Japanese companies in the transactional environment. I define competition as having two levels. On the first, or "lower" level, someone wins and someone loses. Athletic teams battle it out; industries struggle over market shares. On the second, or "higher" level, an objective has been defined which, because of the lower level contest, allows all stakeholder groups to profit in some acceptable way.

Three things, therefore, are required for competition to exist: 1) an upper level *objective* or objectives acceptable to all parties who must obey rules necessary to the lower level contest; 2) *rules* governing the lower level contest that are acceptable to all stakeholders and insure achievement of the accepted upper level objective or objectives; and 3) *a referee* designated to enforce the rules who is acceptable to lower level contestants.

Thus, both winners and losers of athletic contests gain the

upper level objective of salaries, prizes, and/or prestige. They compete according to predefined rules. These rules are enforced by a paid, impartial referee. In terms of Japanese industrial competition, the upper level objective agreed upon by all is advancement of the national interest. The rules of the competition are defined by industry and government together. Government acts as the referee. Because the economic health of the country as a whole is considered more important than personal gain, government decisions are not generally disputed. Individualism is encouraged. Successful men are respected, but only as long as their success profits the whole as well as themselves.

In Japanese industrial society, the conflict, win-lose mode of interaction is found mainly in the contextual environment. It is saved for relations with foreign competitors. Because of the above defined cohesiveness in the internal environment and order in the transactional environment, Japan has been extremely successful in this arena. It and other new industrial powers have cut steadily into markets traditionally dominated by the west. Their share of automobile, electronic equipment, textile, and large ship sales, for example, have been increasing, frequently at the expense of European and U S. business concerns.

WESTERN INDUSTRIAL SOCIETY DEFINES ITS ALTERNATIVES

This attack on the status quo has helped to accentuate the decreasing efficiency of the western industrial process. William Batter says that in 1960 one U.S., two French, or two German industrial workers produced as much as four workers in Japan. In 1980, however, one Japanese worker produced as much as two U.S., two and one-half French or two and one-half German workers.[1] A growing number of major European industries are being nationalized. In the United States many of our giant corporations have become dependent on either government contracts which allow overruns or on direct subsidies. In order for the western free enterprise system to survive, it has become increasingly obvious that major changes must occur. The most pressing of these involves prevailing socioeconomic thought. As usually happens, the required new ingredients have been defined well in advance. As the Industrial Revolution progressed and the amount of physical security available increased, as the number of available jobs grew steadily, as the "welfare net" materialized slowly to provide unemployment compensation, welfare checks, social security, free medical benefits and nutrition for the unfortunate, employees began demanding more from their working lives. In a 1974 survey conducted for the federal government of Canada the majority of subjects, when asked to prioritize a list of job characteristics in terms of importance, responded in the following manner: I) interesting work; 2) means to do it; 3) piece of the action; 4) dignity; 5) good pay; 6) job security.[2] Only unskilled subjects listed good pay and job security above the others.

In a 1978 survey of 23,008 readers conducted by *Psychology Today* magazine, respondents were asked to rank both the importance of and their satisfaction with key job characteristics.[3] In terms of importance, the top 12 were:

1) Chances to do something that makes you feel good about yourself
2) Chances to accomplish something worthwhile
3) Chances to learn something new
4) Opportunity to develop your skills and abilities

5) The amount of freedom you have on your job
6) Chances you have to do things you do best
7) The resources you have to do your job
8) The respect you receive from people you work with
9) Amount of information you get about your job performance
10) Your chances for taking part in making decisions
11) The amount of job security you have
12) The amount of pay you get

Obviously a shift of emphasis has been occurring on all employee levels. Industry is being forced to redefine both desired ends and the means of achieving them. And obviously, as Eric Trist says:

> This transformation [of the work ethic] requires a new philosophy which regards work as a factor fundamental to human development rather than simply a means of earning a living.[4]

IDENTIFYING THE NECESSARY INGREDIENTS

Social scientists began trying to define this new philosophy during the 1960's and 1970's, Based on survey data and case studies they initially attempted to identify job characteristics that would make time spent in the workplace more meaningful and enjoyable. The categories of characteristics developed by Richard Walton, author of "Alienation and Innovation in the Workplace," were considered as comprehensive as any. They included:

1) adequate and fair compensation
2) a safe and healthy work environment
3) opportunity to develop human capabilities
4) opportunity for continuing growth and security
5) positive social integration in the workplace
6) constitutionalism or the protection of workers' rights
7) a positive fit into one's total life space
8) demonstrated social responsibility.[5]

Systems scientists approached the problem from a different direction. While a majority of social scientists worked from "within," identifying work-related needs and important job characteristics, systems scientists worked from "without," trying to define larger, all-encompassing systems of which such needs and characteristics were a part. To be usable, this all-inclusive "systems" framework had to contain exclusive, non-overlapping categories. The psychologist Frederick Herzberg, a pioneer in the effort to define workers' needs, was the first to differentiate between the "extrinsic" and "intrinsic" dimensions of job satisfaction. The extrinsic dimension included "fair and adequate pay, job security, benefits, safety, health and due process." These characteristics related to the employee's tangible job rewards. They defined the worker's share of physical security. The intrinsic dimension, according to Fred Emery of the Wharton School, included "variety and challenge, continuous learning, discretion and autonomy, recognition and support, along with meaningful social contribution and a desirable future."[6] These characteristics related to the employee's intangible job rewards. They defined the worker's ability to derive emotional as well as physical security from his job. At this point in history also, the differentiation between working and non-working or "leisure" hours began breaking down again.

During the Medieval period no such differentiation had existed. The objectives of one's working life had been synonymous with those of one's non-work life. Beginning with the Renaissance, however, work time and leisure time had taken on increasingly different characteristics. One labored at a demeaning task, which produced little emotional security, in older to gain physical security. Work was a necessary evil. During leisure hours one enjoyed the benefits gained from sacrifices made at work. These benefits included a degree of emotional security.

In the modern industrialized world, however, physical security has eventually been assured for a majority of the workforce. As Trist says:

> Though the problem of a new form of scarcity regarding the depletion of non-renewable physical resources has now appeared, this does not mean that the old form of economic scarcity need return. Technology has developed to a point where enough can be produced to provide for the basic (physical) needs of all at a level considerably above that of mere subsistence, at least in technologically advanced countries.[7]

And again, according to U Thant, retired Secretary General of the United Nations:

> The central stupendous truth about developed economies today is that they can have- in anything but the shortest run-the kind and scale of resources they decide to have.... It is no longer resources that limit decisions. It is decisions that make resources.[8]

Employees are now beginning to strive for on-the-job

emotional security as well. Managers and scientists interested in improving the quality of working life have realized the need, as Follet said earlier, to begin viewing work as part of a total life picture.

SOCIO-ECONOMIC DOCTRINE AS THE KEY ISSUE

As a result of this work, new concepts have begun to gain acceptance. The most important, in terms of socio-economic thinking, is the concept of "development," an alternative to that of "growth." "Growth," by definition, has to do with an increase in size or number. It is the yardstick by which we have traditionally measured success in our working lives. In marketplace terms it currently refers to an increase in the quantity of goods available and the ability of people to purchase these goods. For the worker, "growth" relates directly to increase in salary size relative to that of other workers or to the relative increase in his standard of living measured in terms of material possessions and privileges purchasable. "Growth" has more to do with products than processes. It has to do solely with the acquisition of physical security.

"Development," according to Russell Ackoff in his manuscript "On the Nature of Development," is a "process in which an individual increases his ability and desire to satisfy his own [needs and] desires and those of others."[9] Growth in the marketplace is still a necessary condition to achievement of this "increased ability and desire" and will continue to be so for some time. However, though a condition necessary to development, it is far from sufficient. In fact, misdirected *or* overemphasized growth can lead to mal-development, rather than to positive development.

Development, therefore, has to do with processes as well

as products; it has to do with the acquisition of emotional as well as physical security. In the workplace, development is defined in terms of the quality as well as the quantity of goods produced. For the employee it relates to the quality of life achieved during both working and leisure hours. I would further define "development" as a process that allows individuals to gain for themselves and others who might affect their development positively or negatively the physical and emotional security necessary to the discovery and pursuit of a worthwhile purpose in life. People who have a worthwhile purpose feel they are doing something of value, this value being obvious not only to themselves, but to other members of their society. They have been given access to as wide a variety of alternative purposes as the environment permits and have chosen, always retaining the right and ability to change their minds. They have also been given access to education concerning any purpose for which they might develop interest.

A human being is a purposeful system. Purposeful systems are capable of deciding both what they want to achieve (ends) and how they will go about achieving these desired ends (means). Three types of ends exist:

1) GOALS-These include needs and desires that can be satisfied in the short term.

2) OBJECTIVES-These include needs and desires that can be satisfied in the long term.

3) IDEALS- These include needs and desires that the individual knows he has little or no chance of satisfying, but which give direction, impetus, and a sense of importance.

The discovery of a "worthwhile purpose in life" involves all three types of ends. The ideal, however, is the most important. Man must begin with ideals. They provide a standard by which to judge achievement. They give his goals and objectives meaning. It is in the realm of ideals also that we find our sought-after all-inclusive framework of exclusive categories by which to group work-related needs and important job characteristics.

Ancient Greek philosophers designated the pursuit of four key ideals as critical to the achievement of physical and emotional security and to the definition of an acceptable purpose in life. These four ideals—plenty, truth, good, beauty—provide a framework by which to categorize all human needs and desires (see Table 6.1):

1) PLENTY—This category encompasses material needs and desires. It involves pursuit of the steady supply of the goods and services necessary to physical security.

2) TRUTH—This category encompasses intellectual needs and desires. It involves the pursuit of knowledge necessary to the selection and achievement of desirable work and leisure related goals, objectives, and ideals.

3) GOOD—This category encompasses moral needs and desires. It involves the pursuit of assurances that a fair deal will be received, that one will gain credit when credit is due and will not be victimized by superiors or peers.

4) BEAUTY - This category encompasses sensual needs and desires. It involves the pursuit of contentment and excitement in life, contentment resulting from a pleasing, nonthreatening work and leisure environment which soothes the senses, excitement resulting from the availability of challenge, newness, and adventure which stimulate the senses.

As we see in Table 4.1, both Walton's and Emery's categories of key job characteristics fit readily into this larger, all-inclusive framework .

TABLE 4.1 Fit Between Greek Developmental Ideals and Walton's and Emery's Categories of Key Job Characteristics

PLENTY (Material Needs)	Adequate and Fair Compensation A Safe and Healthy Work Environment	WALTON
	Fair and Adequate Pay Job Security Benefits Safety Health	EMERY
TRUTH (Intellectual Needs)	Opportunity to Develop Human Capabilities	WALTON
	Continuous Learning	EMERY
GOOD (Moral Needs)	Positive Social Integration in Workplace Constitutionalism / Protection of Rights Demonstrated Social Responsibility	WALTON
	Due Process Discretion and Autonomy Recognition and Support Meaningful Social Contribution	EMERY
BEAUTY (Sensual Needs)	A Positive Fit Into One's Total Lifespace	WALTON
	Variety and Challenge A Desirable Future	EMERY

Thus, the logic for the necessary new socio-economic doctrine has begun to appear. Rather than replacing, it absorbs and makes the old doctrine part of a much richer whole which stresses emotional as well as physical security. It also encourages cooperation. Resources required for the "production" of truth, good, and beauty, are largely non-material and, therefore, limitless. The amounts of truth, good, and beauty made available depend largely on man's desire and ability to generate them. Cooperation is obviously the best vehical for such endeavors.

Even, however, when emphasis remains on competition, results in these latter three realms can be positive. In terms of development, I do not lose if an associate proves he has more knowledge than I about a certain topic. He must do so by telling me something I don't know, by teaching me. In order to win, therefore, he must enhance my development. Neither am I beaten in the modern day workplace by a peer who gains a "fairer" deal than I. First, such deals are normally accomplished by group efforts. Second, once defined, it is difficult to deny the same deal to any legitimate stakeholder. Finally, when someone improves the esthetic dimension of a situation by making it more calming or exciting, everyone involved usually profits.

HOW CHANGES IN SOCIO-ECONOMIC DOCTRINE ARE AFFECTING MANAGEMENT THEORY

The above defined changes in doctrine and the attendant cooperative ethic encourage a smoother transition to a more useful decision making paradigm in the workplace. Middle management's role, in particular, will be affected. Rather than bosses who solve production problems, middle managers will become facilitators and coordinators. By "facilitator" I mean that middle managers will begin to use interpersonal and group skills to facilitate a participative problem solving process. By "coordinator" I mean that middle managers will help lower level employees gain the resources needed to deal adequately with technical and socio system problems. These resources include information, money, time, feedback, and emotional support. Thus, middle management will begin to function as Likert's "linchpin" between production problem solvers on lower levels and strategic planners on the higher. In order to play this role effectively, it will be involved in both processes. Middle managers will learn to coordinate mission statement, objectives, and goal definition with the realities of the shop or office floor.

Thus, as we see, because of modern day pressures and our shift back toward a cooperative ethic, a historic synthesis is, in fact, occurring. During the Medieval period employees from all levels possessed roughly the same expertise and participated in a joint problem solving effort. During the early Industrial Revolution management "experts" controlled the necessary information and dominated the process while the majority of employees had no say. Now, during the late Industrial Revolution, because of the increasing sophistication of industrial systems, "experts" are found in all departments, on all levels, and in all environments. They are being called on to pool their social and technical system knowledge in joint efforts to solve problems much too multifaceted for any one individual or level to unravel. We have progressed, therefore, from decision making by groups through decision making by *experts* and finally to decision making by *groups* of *experts*.

During the most recent stages of this progression, however, another complication has arisen, one that will cause drastic changes, not only in the decision making process itself, but in the very nature of work and the workplace. In Chapter Seven I shall address this complication, introducing an entirely new and unusual participant in organizational activities.

SUMMARY

Two things occurred during the latter part of the Industrial Revolution to encourage change in traditional management processess. First, new industrial powers began to gain control of a growing share of both foreign and domestic markets. The Japanese especially, having learned from the West's mistakes, developed a more efficient, participative decision making process based on a cooperative ethic at the individual business level and a competitive ethic at the industrial sector level.

Second, western socio-economic thinking began to shift. Physical security had been achieved by a majority of employees. They were now beginning to seek emotional security as well. People began to talk about "development" rather than simply "growth." While growth had traditionally involved conflict over limited resources, those necessary to development were largely limitless. The most efficient means of achieving the objectives of development, therefore, was cooperation.

Society had again discovered the necessary rationalization and vehicle for change in its decision making paradigm. The participative process that evolved as a result, however, differed from that found during the Medieval era. A synthesis had, in fact, occurred. Individuals (Renaissance, Reformation, Early Industrial Revolution) with expertise in different areas now pooled their talents in a cooperative (Medieval period) effort attempting to understand and deal effectively with increasingly sophisticated issues concerning organizational structure, function, and environments. But still our presentation is not up to date. In Chapter Five we see that technology has recently provided us with a new participant, a new challenge. This participant has, indeed, set off a second Industrial Revolution, one that is beginning to restructure and re-orient, once again, management theory.

NOTES

1. William Batter, "Productivity and the Working Environment," The Wharton School of the University of Pennsylvania Dean's Lecture Series.
2. Eric Trist, "The Quality of Working Life and Organizational Improvement." Unpublished, Management and Behavioral Science Center, The Wharton School, October 1979, pp. 3-4.
3. Patricia Renwick and Edward Lawler, "What You Really Want From Your Job," *Psychology Today, May* 1978, p. 56.
4. Trist, p. 7.
5. J. Lloyd Suttle, "Improving Life at Work—Problems and Prospects," in *Improving Life at Work*, J. Richard Hackman and J. Lloyd Suttle (Santa Monica, Calif.: Goodyear Publishing Co., 1977), pp. 3-4.
6. Eric Trist, "The Evolution of Socio-Technical Systems," *Issues in the Quality of Working Life.* No. 2, Ontario Quality of Working Life Center, June 1981, p. 30.
7. Trist, "The Quality of Working Life and Organizational Improvement," p. 3 .
8. Alvin Toffler, *Future Shock, p. .17*
9. Russell Ackoff, "Prologue to National Development Planning." Unpublished, Busch Center, The Wharton School, 1983.

5

The Post-Industrial Revolution, Part I

TECHNOLOGY AS THE KEY ISSUE

We have watched the definition of key period variables come full circle. During the pre-Industrial Revolution era change in socio-economic thinking was the major issue. The pre-Industrial Revolution era, as defined, had three parts. During the first, the Medieval period, community service was more important than self aggrandizement. Emphasis was on cooperation and the achievement of emotional security. This situation changed gradually during the second part, the Renaissance, until, during the third, the Reformation, the individual reigned supreme. Emphasis shifted to conflict and the achievement of physical security, no matter what the cost in terms of human suffering.

During the early Industrial Revolution technology became the major issue. Machine-like efficiency was the objective. Socio systems were designed as extensions of technical ones. Emphasis remained on conflict.

During the middle Industrial Revolution era size/organizational design emerged as a key issue. Businesses were becoming too large and complex to be run efficiently in the

66

traditional, bureaucratic manner. Although the need for change in organizational design became increasingly apparent, management generally attempted to rationalize their situation instead of adapting. Marketplace pressures became the main issue during the first part of the late Industrial Revolution era. Asian competitors who had learned from western society's mistakes and adapted more effectively to the rapidly changing environment were beating us in both foreign and domestic markets. To remain competitive, change was obviously necessary in our management philosophy. Socio-economic thinking, therefore, once again emerged and began replacing marketplace pressures as the focal issue during the latter part of the late Industrial Revolution era.

Thus, up to this point we have spun from doctrine to technology to organization size/design to marketplace pressures and back to doctrine as the key variable. According to this cycle, emphasis, at least during the early part of the post-Industrial Revolution era, should fall, once again, on technology. And it does. I insinuated strongly in Chapter One that I believe major changes in socio-economic thinking and technology have been interdependent. During the pre-Industrial Revolution era technological improvements that facilitated the accumulation of wealth by some, frequently at the expense of others, were made more acceptable by the timely arrival of the Protestant Work Ethic and its interpretations. This new doctrine appears to have evolved or to have been molded as a means of making the situation spawned by the new technology socially acceptable.

As the late Industrial Revolution progresses into the post-Industrial Revolution, we again see linkages between a newly evolving doctrine and a new technology. We have defined the new doctrine in Chapter Four. The new technology is the computer.

EVOLUTIONARY STAGES OF THE TECHNICAL SYSTEM

"Tools" and "Machines," their more sophisticated progeny, have passed through three important evolutionary stages and are now well into a fourth.

1. Prior to the Industrial Revolution, man or animals generally supplied the power required for the production process. Craftsmen defined both desired outputs and required inputs. They transformed inputs with their own hands, using tools to facilitate their work.

2. During the early Industrial Revolution other machines generated the bulk of the power required. Man again defined both desired outputs and required inputs. He designed the machines which transformed the inputs. He controlled the production process directly by making specification adjustments and by pushing the button or pulling the lever that activated the machine.

3. During the middle and late Industrial Revolution other machines generated the bulk of the power required. Man defined desired outputs and, with the help of machines, required inputs. He designed the machine, generally a switchboard or panel of electric circuitry capable of sending a variety of signals, which transformed the inputs. He controlled the production process indirectly through this switchboard or panel.

4. During the post-Industrial Revolution other machines continue to generate the bulk of the power required. Man and machines together define desired outputs and required inputs. Man has built "parent" machines capable of designing, controlling the manufacture of, and running generations of production machines. These machines are able to organize information in a way that allows achievement of a predefined

goal or objective. The "parent" machines are, again, computers. ENIAC, the world's first electronic digital computer, was completed in 1946. It filled a room and weighed thirty tons. Advances in solid state circuit component technology preceded the arrival of inexpensive minicomputers during the late 1960's and the 1970's. By the mid- 1960's most large businesses had turned to computers to facilitate such tasks as controlling inventory, storing payroll data, and issuing checks. During this same period engineers at the General Electric Corporation began using computers to help design component parts.

The next step was to organize the flow of information between functional areas on a factory floor with computers. Eventually they were used also to store, retrieve, and transport materials; to process materials; and to run robots that completed repetitive tasks such as spot welding, assembly, and painting.

The modern microprocessor, "a computer on a chip," can endow a machine with decision-making ability, a memory for instructions, and a range of self-adjusting controls.

In terms of the future, at least one organization, the Ministry for International Trade and Industry in Japan, expects to have a "thinking" computer by 1990. This machine will react to human speech as well as written data. It will ask questions, draw inferences, and make judgments "based on knowledge of word meanings as well as numbers." It will also be capable of learning by "recalling and studying its errors."[1]

SHORT-TERM EFFECTS OF COMPUTER TECHNOLOGY ON BUSINESSES

Obviously, the advent and development of computer technology has had a profound effect on the workplace. Computerized equipment is redefining the nature of jobs in all three traditional sectors of the economy manufacturing, services, and agriculture.

In the manufacturing sector robots, or "iron collar workers," are becoming increasing popular on the factory floor. According to Laura Conigliano, a leading robotics analyst, there are approximately 6,000 robots in use in the united States today. By 1990 she estimates that there will be 150,000.[2] The robot's performance, though rarely faster than that of the laborer, never varies. Also, robots never tire, get moody, have to go to the bathroom, suffer from "hostile" environments, or walk off the job. All they need to change tasks is a new tool attached to the end of their arm and a new program in their chip. While the cost of human labor continues to increase, that of robot technology is decreasing. In the automobile industry, for example, while the cost of human labor had climbed to approximately $14 per hour by January 1980, the cost of robot labor was approximately $4.80 per hour. This latter cost included installation, maintenance, depreciation, and energy.[3] Automation, therefore, is increasing both the quantity and quality of industrial production while, at the same time, decreasing cost.

In the "factory of the future" being designed at West Berlin's Technological University, robots are part of a multisector, almost totally automated production process incorporating:

1) Minicomputers which regulate small cells of robot-fed machine tools, providing, in the process, quality control and routine maintenance.
2) Larger central computers which control the flow of work and materials.
3) A third sector of computers capable of designing new parts.
4) A system which relays breakdown signals from cell computers to the central computer allowing it to reorganize overall plant production schedules.

Employees play three roles in this system:

1) planners/optimizers of the production process,
2) computer operators who work with the production cell computers,
3) technologists who help with maintenance and the manufacture of new machine components.[4]

According to Thomas Gunn of Arthur D. Little, however, it is not the production process that provides the greatest opportunity for increasing output through the use of improved technology. Instead, this opportunity is found in the organizing, scheduling, and managing of the total operation; in the meshing of design, management, and manufacturing information into a universally available network.[5] The development of such networks is changing the nature of management and white collar responsibilities. Vincent Guiliano, also of Arthur D. Little, defines the evolution of the business office in terms of three historic stages:

1. Pre-Industrial Office—Little systemic organization existed. People did their jobs independently, had their own style. Human interaction was important.

2. Industrial Office—Modeled on the production line. Tasks were fragmented and standardized. Documents entered one end of the flow line and emerged from the other. Work was dull. Errors were hard to correct as a result of the subdivision of tasks because no one had a complete answer. Personal interaction was minimized and standardized. Emphasis was on efficiency.

3. Information Age Office—Combines terminal based work stations, a continuous updated data base, and communications to achieve a high level of efficiency along with a return to people centered work. The equipment is paced to the worker instead of vice versa. Rather than handling one or several steps in a process, the worker handles all customer-related activities in a number of accounts. Productivity is a measure of customer satisfaction rather than hours worked or items produced.[6]

Many of the above defined changes are also occurring in the service sector, which now employs nearly 70 percent of the U.S. workforce. The health care industry is computerizing much of its diagnostic and office work. The banking industry is computerizing customer service. The shipping of goods in containers has allowed a large degree of automation in the freight industry. Educational institutions are now using computers not only for administrative work, but to teach.

As an example of what is happening in the agricultural sector, a friend of mine recently paid a winter visit to a dairy farm. The morning alter his arrival he rose early, ready to help milk and feed the herd. Instead of the barn, however, the farmer led him to an adjacent shack. Throwing open the doors, the farmer revealed an elaborate control panel from which he milked, fed, monitored, turned out, played music to, and generally tended his herd in a fraction of the time previously consumed by such chores.

SHORT-TERM EFFECTS OF COMPUTER TECHNOLOGY ON THE JOB MARKET

Short-term effects of this new technology on the manufacturing sector job market tend to be alarming. In this sector component parts production engages approximately 40 percent of the total workforce. According to Fred Emery, "microprocessors could replace 80 percent of that 40 percent within three to five years, once the process was started."[7] A Carnegie-Mellon study estimates that first generation robots possessing mechanical dexterity will ultimately replace approximately 1.2 million blue collar workers in the United States alone. Second generation robots which possess external sensing abilities as well will eventually replace approximately 3.8 million more, while future generations of robots possessing "intelligence," the ability to "self-diagnose," and more easily replaced components will sharply reduce need for the technicians comprising the majority of the workforce in West Berlin's "Factory of the Future."[8]

Similar trends are forecast for white collar positions and the service sector. Guiliano says that "white collar staff reductions of as much as 50 percent have been common in companies which have instituted the information age system."[9] Though the number of service sector jobs has grown steadily in recent decades, many of these .are now being threatened by the same forces that threaten manufacturing sector jobs.

The agricultural sector, which at one time employed 70 percent of the U.S. workforce, now, due mainly to automation, employs only 3 percent. The microprocessor has been the latest contributor to this attrition.

And finally, overall, Jenkins and Sherman forecast that the British force will suffer a reduction of 23.2 percent by the year

2000.[10] Many consider this estimate conservative in terms of not only Britain, but all industrialized western countries.

LONG-TERM EFFECTS OF COMPUTER TECHNOLOGY ON THE JOB MARKET

A critical question, or I should say *the* critical question concerning the post-Industrial Revolution is "If this new technology is ultimately capable of automating a significant percentage of current and future jobs in our economy, what will happen to the workers?"

Traditional reasoning has been that automation, while initially causing worker displacement, eventually creates new jobs. In terms of the microprocessor revolution, however, this might not prove true. Previous new technology has replaced the worker at only one stage of a total process. In manufacturing this process ranges from raw material collection to marketing and sales. In the service sector it ranges from the definition of a need to the delivery of services. At the same time, previous new technology has increased the number of jobs at other stages in the process. It has also bred new products and new employment opportunities.

The microprocessor's greatest value is that it can coordinate and run all stages in a specific process. It can also integrate and run a collection of related processes. Thus, jobs are lost all along the line. Wassily Leontief of New York University describes the situation as follows:

> Beginning with the invention of the steam engine, successive waves of technological innovation have brought in the now industrialized or "developed" countries a spectacular growth of both employment and real wages, a combination

74

that spells prosperity and social peace....
There are signs today, however, that past experience cannot serve as a reliable guide to the future of technological change. With the advent of solid state electronics, machines that have been displacing human muscle are being succeeded by machines that take over functions of the human nervous system, not only in production but in the service industries as well.[11]

We first developed machines capable of physically manufacturing goods and services. We are now developing machines capable of controlling entire manufacturing systems. The latest wave of new technology will surely, once again, make possible an increasing array of products and options. These new products, however, will also probably be designed, manufactured, sold, and delivered by computer based technology.

REDEFINING THE HUMAN ROLE IN MODERN BUSINESS

What, then, is the role, if any, left for man in the creation of "plenty"? Or maybe we should first ask, "What *can't* a microprocessor do'." It can definitely solve standard operational problems, but is that all? Could the microprocessor be capable of creative problem solving as well? Hubert Dreyfus, author of *What Computers Can't DO*, says no. He believes that computers are, in fact, "sort of a fancy calculation machine which just applies a whole bunch of rules to a whole bunch of facts." He says that they do very well in their restricted domains but are incompetent in any other domain. They cannot generalize or learn.[12]

Is it possible, however, that, as the Japanese Minister for International Trade and Industry says, microprocessors will eventually be capable of at least the latter process? Will they some day be able to improve on the efforts of their programmers, both enhancing the efficiency of and supplementing the logic placed in their system? And can this ability to learn, if achieved, give them the capacity for creative problem solving as well'?

I believe that the above argument depends primarily on the definition of "creativity" used. Most research concerning "creativity" takes one of three approaches. The first includes case studies of men and women popularly believed to have performed creative acts. An example would be the widely acclaimed account of the French mathematician Henri Poincare's activities preceding his definition of the Fuchsian functions. Such case studies, however, focus on the process that led to the "act." The properties that made the act itself "creative" by some universal standard are not defined in a way that allows useful measurement in group testing situations.

The second approach is to define and compare the personality traits of men and women involved in careers or pursuits considered creative. An attempt is made to discover which traits are most frequently possessed by these people. In such studies, again, an operational definition of the concept being explored is usually missing. The decision about what constitutes a creative career or pursuit is largely subjective.

The third approach is to ask subjects to answer creativity testing questionnaires or to attempt to solve creativity testing puzzles/ problems. What makes the involved puzzles or problems "creativity testing" is again not clearly defined. Correct answers or solutions, theoretically, necessitate possession of more than average levels of those traits previously identified in people considered to have performed creative acts or considered to be pursuing creative careers—fluency, receptivity, flexibility, and so forth. What researchers in this third category have been talking about, however, is actually problem solving ability that might be creative.

An operational definition of human creativity which synthesizes key ingredients identified in the literature is that offered by Elsa Vergara of the Wharton School:

> Creativity: The ability of a subject in a choice situation to modify self-imposed constraints so as to enable him to select courses of action or produce outcomes that he would not otherwise select or produce, and which are more efficient for or valuable to him than any he would otherwise have chosen.[13]

This definition, however, is still ultimately questionable. One would require a thorough understanding of a subject's psyche at the moment of choice to truly differentiate between a creative and noncreative act. An isolated individual in a society where the wheel has been used for years might never have seen one and might eventually "re-invent the wheel." This would be a creative act for him. On the other hand, that individual might also, at some point, have caught a glimpse of a wheel and registered the concept subconsciously. In this case his "invention" would not involve creativity. The researcher would need the ability to plumb the depths of the subject's memory in order to discover the truth.

Thee only events that can, without doubt, be labeled "creative" are those that have never before occurred within the recorded history of man. Poincare's achievement would fit into this category, as would Einstein's definition of the theory

77

of relativity. Creativity, in fact, has to do with flexibility of thought or emotion. It involves organizing available information or concepts in a new way that enhances understanding. Everyone is potentially creative. As Douglas Hofstadter, a staff writer for *Scientific American*, says, "Creativity is part of the fabric of all human thought, rather than some esoteric, rare, exceptional or fluky by-product of the ability to think." If the above is true, microprocessors capable of "learning from their mistakes" should ultimately be capable of generating creative solutions to problems. Hofstadter agrees. He continues, "I see creativity and insight as being intimately bound up with intelligence and so I cannot imagine a noncreative yet intelligent machine."[14]

Obviously, however, existing definitions cannot be used to measure the creativity of a machine. Because we have studied only our own creativity, we have framed our definitions in terms of human beings, automatically denying such potential in any other system, animate or inanimate. The microprocessor has no "self imposed constraints" to overcome. It will do only what it has been programmed to do. A programmer might give his computer the capability of organizing available information or concepts in a new way that improves understanding. The computer, therefore, will be capable of generating unique problem solutions. But it will accomplish this feat only because it has been programmed to do so by a human.

LONG-TERM EFFECTS OF COMPUTER TECHNOLOGY ON BUSINESS SOCIAL SYSTEMS

Actually, creativity is not, in my mind, the main issue. The main issue, as was hinted at in the above discussion of the microprocessor's creative potential, is purpose. I mentioned purpose when offering my concept of human development in Chapter Four. One difference, also previously mentioned, exists between humans and machines that machines will probably never overcome. Humans are "purposeful" systems, whereas machines are only "purposive." A purposeful system, as we have said earlier, is one capable of defining its own purpose and of changing that definition whenever desired, no matter what the environmental circumstances. A purposive system is one that must have its purpose define by an outside force, always, ultimately, man

While, therefore, a majority of the technical problems (means problems) faced during the post-lndustrial Revolution will most effectively be dealt with by the new, automated technicians, man must address related ends problems. He must define the purpose computers will serve. He must deal with problems concerning the definition of his organization's mission, objectives, and goals. He must also continue to address problems in the organization's socio systems. These systems are composed of "purposeful" individuals and groups of "purposeful" individuals. Computers, being "purposive," do not enjoy the flexibility required to deal adequately with such systems. As Lee Dembart of the Los Angeles Times Service says, Machines are incapable of developing true "appreciation for the human condition, for what people acquire as part of being human."

Dreyfus agrees, "You can't put in the shared understanding of human concerns and purposes that embodies society."[15] And, of course, future employees must deal with problems concerning the relationship between "purposeful" socio and "purposive" technical systems. Examples of the above types of problems would include: I) What goods should be produced? 2) What efforts should be made by the company to assist employees in adapting to the post-Industrial Revolution work environment? and 3) What type of organizational design would be most productive in terms of both social and technical system objectives?

Because of the coincidental and complementary shift in socio- economic thinking defined in Chapter Four, employees will also begin to address a wide range of problems in the organization's contextual environment. The reason for the expanding focus will be discussed in Chapter Six

SUMMARY

I have come full circle in my definition of key period variables and have started what appears to be a second, more compacted round. During the latter part of the late Industrial Revolution era socio-economic thinking reemerged as the focus. During the first part of the post Industrial Revolution era technology has regained the spotlight, though it seems to enjoy a necessary symbiotic relationship with socio-economic thinking.

The new technology which is currently revolutionizing the nature of work is the microprocessor. This "computer on a chip" is displacing an increasing number of workers in all three major economic sectors—manufacturing, services, agriculture. Although, traditionally, more efficient machines have ultimately increased the overall number of jobs available, the microprocessor might not. This machine has the potential, not only of completing repetitious tasks more efficiently than humans, but also of controlling entire processes.

In terms of problem solving, microprocessors are capable of producing "creative" solutions if programmed to do so when one accepts a more generalized definition of creativity than those offered by most social scientists. Microprocessors are not, however, capable of defining their own purpose. Man must do this. Microprocessors will also probably never achieve the flexibility required to address adequately socio systems problems.

The future role of employees in the workplace, therefore, will be mainly to deal with issues involving purpose. Problems addressed will include the most appropriate uses of modern technology; the most efficient definition of organizational mission, objectives, goals; the identification of appropriate social system interaction; and specification of the most profitable relationship between social and technical systems.

In Chapter Five, then. I have identified the modern technology that has become a key issue and discussed its potential impact on the workplace. Next, I must explore the new lifestyles being encouraged by the combined effects of this new technology and previously defined changes in modern day socio-economic thinking. This will be my task in Chapter Six.

NOTES

1. Allen Boriako, "The Chip," *National Geographic, Vol.* 162, No. 4, October 1982, p. 421.

2. Alix Freeman, "Behind Every Successful Robot Is a Technician," *Career's* 83, pp. 34-35.

3. "Some Lessons for the Decade Ahead: New Hands in the Workplace—The Robot," U.S. *News and World Report,* January 21, 1980, pp. 73-74.

4. David Clutterbuck, "The Future of Work," *International Management,* August 1979, p. 19.

5. Thomas Gunn, "The Mechanization of Design and Manufacturing," *Scientific American,* September 1982, p. 115.

6. Vincent Guiliano, "The Mechanization of Office Work," *Scientific American,* September 1982, p. 162.

7. Fred Emery, "The Fifth Wave? Embarking on the Next Forty Years," Unpublished, May 1979, p. 15.

8. Freeman, p. 34.

9. Guiliano, p. 163.

10. Eric Trist, *The Evolution of Socio-Technical Systems,* Ontario Quality of Working Life Centre, June 1981, p. 50.

11. Wassily Leontief, "The Distribution of Work and Income," *Scientific American,* September 1982, p. 188

12. Lee Dembart, "Expert Computers Raising Questions," *Philadelphia Inquirer,* Sunday, December 12, 1982, p. 5-D.

13. Russell Ackoff and Elsa Vergara, "Creativity in Problem Solving and Planning: A Review," *European Journal of Operations Research,* Vol. 7, 1981, p. 1

14. Douglas Hofstadter, "Metamagical Themas," *Scientific American,* September 1982, p. 18.

15. Dembart, p. 5-D

6

The Post-Industrial Revolution, Part II

POTENTIAL FOR DISASTER

The results of large scale automation, of course, could be disastrous. The French mystic Jacques Ellul, author of the popular book The *Technological Society*, along with others, has been predicting such a scenario for some time. The direct predictions of Karl Marx, the nineteenth century German philosopher credited with defining the theory of modern socialism, could come true. Marx believed that the capitalist system would perish once newer and more powerful machines had "driven such a large portion of the labor force out of work that producers would no longer have enough consumers to buy the goods their machines were spewing out."[1] The post-Industrial Revolution is, in one sense, Marx's dream come true. If my above discussed suspicions are correct, machines will, indeed, displace workers without creating new jobs. Were doctrinal emphasis, at the same time, to revert to an exclusive quest for plenty, Marx's disaster would have a good chance of occurring. Those who owned and controlled the increasingly productive technology would grow extremely powerful while the majority of the population became dependent for survival on government support and/or corporate largess. The ethic that accompanies cultural emphasis on plenty would make this situation unbearable. Strife would most likely erupt. The system would either self-destruct under the pressure of mass unemployment or become totalitarian.

Chances of the above scenario materializing, however, are currently diminishing. Modern technological and social forces defined in previous chapters are encouraging the materialization of a more realistic and positive future in the workplace.

EDUCATION COMES TO THE FORE

One of the key ingredients of this future is education, which has come a long way. Schools in Europe during the Medieval era were controlled by the church. They catered strictly to future priests, lawyers, civil servants, and businessmen from upper class families. Commoners received no education. As populations, urban centers, and commerce grew, however, the need for people in other segments of the society to be able to read and write increased. Employees realized the value of being able to read notices posted in the guild hall and town square, of being able to keep accounts, and write letters. By 1350, guilds and other community organizations had begun establishing their own elementary schools. To facilitate the process, governments and businesses replaced Latin with the vernacular as their official language. Invention of the printing press in 1450 helped greatly by making written material available to the general public. Books once read only by clergy and the nobility were soon translated from Latin and sold to commoners.

The Protestant Revolution made one of its objectives the provision of elementary education for the faithful. The movement's various branches placed great importance on the ability of parishioners from all social levels to read the Scriptures in private At Luther's and Calvin's urging children were compelled to attend primary school in order that the good of society might be served through development of their potential. Compulsory education began in Germany during the mid-1500's and spread to other countries.

England, as I have mentioned before, was the exception. The Reformation here was mainly a political rather than a religious movement. The Catholic school system was shut down and not replaced. Education once again became a privilege for those who could afford it. Due to this laissez-faire attitude, England trailed continental European countries by one-half century in providing universal elementary education. Secondary schools were not available to all until the beginning of the twentieth century.

The eighteenth and nineteenth centuries saw three movements that influenced mass education greatly and laid the foundations for our modern institutions. The first was a new liberalism and idealism evolving from scientific and philosophical advances. Once man had discovered that his earth was not the center of the universe, not the sole focus of God's attention and not totally under God's control, he felt more able to affect his destiny. Social institutions, by definition, had been created to meet his needs. They should be organized to do so in the most effective manner. Man could help define such effectiveness: he no longer had to depend solely on the word of God and God's representatives for such definitions. Comenius of Austria, Condorcet of France,

85

Pestalozzi and Rousseau of Switzerland, and Jefferson of the United States helped redefine education during this period of enlightenment as a means of developing human potential, as an avenue through which society could improve itself. The second movement was nationalism. Nationalistic policies began to evolve in Europe when governments replaced the church as the primary power and realized the importance of controlling both sources of raw materials and markets. It was mainly with the French Revolution, however, that nationalistic policies began to influence education positively. The Revolution freed peasants from feudal obligations, expanded suffrage, and made men equal before the law. It also aligned the old-order European countries against France. This combination of factors convinced the French government to use education as a means of creating a national solidarity. The masses should be informed of the advantages enjoyed under the new regime. History, geography, and civics were added to the curriculum. An effort was made to encourage citizens to adopt one national language. Napoleon Bonaparte, the leader of both France's armies and state, also improved secondary school and university systems, creating, in the process, the first national administration for education called the "University of France."

The third movement was the Industrial Revolution. At its outset the Revolution was harmful to the advancement of public education, especially in England where it both began and reached its greatest intensity. First, it destroyed the apprenticeship system which had frequently included the teaching of more than technical skills. Second, it put children to work at a very young age. They had no time for school. It is estimated that in 1870, at the height of England's dominance as an industrial power, only two-fifths of its children between the ages of six and ten and only one-third of those between the ages of ten and twelve were attending school.[2] Eventually, however, as we have shown in Chapter Two, the Revolution not only encouraged education of the masses, but made it imperative.

Concerning the future of education, Daniel Berg, Dean of Science at the Carnegie-Mellon Institute, says that, "With automation eliminating many unskilled jobs, workers are going to have to work smarter, not harder, and be able to adjust quickly to fast changing technologies."[3] Kenneth Huddleston and Dorothy Fenwick, in their article, "The Productivity Challenge: Business/Education Partnership," estimate that as a result of the current technological revolution "... from 20 percent to 80 percent of the workers at the average company will need retraining."[4] And finally. Fred Emery predicts that:

> Western societies are likely to come much closer to McLuhan's suggestion that work will be learning.... When a new, automated plant is brought into production it is more possible and economically desirable to design the task of operators and managers so that the performance of the plant (staff) will reflect a learning curve over its entire operating life This is only possible when the chosen structure places a premium on learning, experimenting, and problem solving. The pressure toward greater productivity will hasten these changes....[5]

The traditional constraints are beginning to fade. During the pre-Industrial Revolution era an extremely small percentage of the population received more than an elementary level education. During the Industrial Revolution this gradually changed until, with the post-Industrial Revolution era, not only does an increasingly large percentage of the population receive college and graduate level degrees, but continuing education is coming into vogue.

Because of demands imposed by the constantly accelerating rate of environmental change, also because of the increased opportunity offered by growing amounts of leisure time and by the expanding number and variety of facilities, education is becoming an ongoing, integral part of life rather than an activity upon which one focuses during a specific, highly structured period of one's childhood, adolescence, and young adult years. Also, education is now gained, not only in the classroom, but from computers, television, tapes, consultants, "working" vacations, amusement facilities, magazines, newspapers, classrooms on wheels, and so forth.

Thus, the traditional boundaries of "time," "place," and "technique" are crumbling. Education is becoming a more fluid, continuous experience. It is also becoming a major growth industry. A rapidly increasing, number of companies are currently developing their own educational efforts on lower as well as higher levels. At the lower levels they are attempting mainly to compensate for the weaknesses of the traditional system by offering courses in English, mathematics, and other basic skills to employees during working hours. The Continental Bank of Chicago, for example, instructs clerical workers two hours a day twice a week for 24 weeks in the basics of English. The bank also offers a ten hour numbers skills course.[6]

In terms of higher education, most current efforts are being made in conjunction with colleges and universities. This partnership has resulted in "customized training courses, industrial testing career development programs, quality circle training, training needs analysis, and state-of-the-art seminars." The number of such joint ventures is increasing rapidly. In 1981, for example, more such programs were established than during the previous five years.[7]

The types of arrangement involved includes: 1) on-site use of academic personnel to train employees: 2) use of business personnel in the university classroom; 3) a mixture of the above two alternatives called "cooperative education"; 4) the joint development and use of facilities; and 5) joint research ventures.[8]

In 1973 a report financed by the Carnegie Corporation showed how much high level education was already going on in U.S. corporations, unions, and governmental organizations. As a result, a system was developed to allow the awarding of college credits for courses meeting standards defined by professional educators.[9] The added incentive for employees is obvious.

TECHNOLOGY AIDS THE TRANSITION

Thus, the new technology is both indirectly and directly supporting the materialization of a positive future in the workplace. Indirectly, it is making increased levels of employee education necessary. These increased levels of education are, at the same time, helping workers to better pursue personal development. This trend is especially obvious in the service sector where according to Eli Ginzberg of Columbia University:

> Work has more dimensions and complexities than factory work, particularly considering the much higher proportion of professional, scientific, and technical people employed in service industries. It is the hallmark of such personnel that their training has conditioned them to decide what work to do, how to do it, and even when to do it.... There is a growing tension between the traditional hierar-

chical structure of organizations and the implicit (and increasingly explicit) demands of professionals for greater autonomy in their work..[10]

Directly, the new technology has the potential of making work more interesting. Unfortunately, some businesses, still focused on efficiency alone, are using it solely to improve job segmentation and simplification techniques developed during the early Industrial Revolution. One has only to observe a fast food chain operation to understand this. Young people mainly scurry about like robots on fixed tracks or stand at a station cooking the same hamburger, filling the same order again and again. Bored managers with equally precise job descriptions try to maintain a stern but friendly demeanor as they insist that the human machine parts don't slack off. These employees must sympathize with the descriptive comment made by an assembly line worker in the 1940's:

> There is nothing more discouraging than having a barrel beside you with 10,000 bolts (doughnuts) in it and using them all up. Then you get another barrel with another 10,000 bolts (doughnuts) and you know that every one of those 10,000 bolts (doughnuts) has to be picked up and put in exactly the same place as the last 10,000 bolts (doughnuts).
> [11]

As an increasing number of people begin to define their potential as purposeful systems, however, and as the price of automation continues to drop, the quality of working life will continue to improve. At least that part of the esthetic ideal (beauty) that involves excitement will become available during working hours as well as after. Because more "dirty" jobs will be automated and because employees will exercise more control over their environment, the amount of contentment achieved will also increase. At the same time the worker's increased degree of education, along with his greater responsibility, will allow him to better assure that he receives a fair break.

My conclusion, therefore, is that as the potential of the post-Industrial Revolution unfolds, all levels of the workforce, instead of just a paycheck (ideal of plenty), will begin seeking and securing continuous education opportunity (ideal of truth), greater control over their situation (ideal of good), and more stimulating work in a more relaxed environment (ideal of beauty). We shall see a growing effort in the economic sector to make total human development an integral part of one's work as well as leisure life.

WHAT TO DO WITH THE UNEMPLOYED

I have previously stated and documented my belief that machines will replace a significant percentage of current and future jobs. I have also explained why I think this change will help improve the situation of those still employed. But what about Marx's displaced masses? How will their development be affected by the above defined changes?

First, it is necessary to define the nature of future unemployment. A clear differentiation between those with jobs and those without may not be possible for long. Changes in socio-economic thinking have helped create alternatives. Several of these alternatives are based on the fact that a growing number of workers are willing to sacrifice pay for more free time. According to a recent U.S. Department of Labor study, such employees, "depending on their age group, family status, occupation and so on, would be prepared to forgo a certain fraction of their current income in exchange

91

for extended vacation allotments, sabbaticals, early retirement or shorter work weeks."[12] This attitude has also been observed in European countries. It is encouraged there by the fact that supplemental benefits are frequently paid to "those who work fewer than the normal number of hours per week."[13]

The implication again is that once a certain degree of physical security is achieved, emphasis begins swinging again toward emotional needs. Once employees are satisfied with the salary received, they begin to seek more free time during which to enjoy the benefits derived. A 1979 University of Michigan Survey Research Center study showed that while only 30 percent of the workers polled thought themselves underpaid, 55 percent wanted more time off. In that same year a group of "rank and file" union members banded together to form an "All Union Committee to Shorten the Work Week." Their goal was a 35 hour work week as a national standard instead of the somewhat less than 42 hour one which has existed since World War II.[14]

According to Dr. Mario Unnia of Prospecta Sarl, the number of part-time workers employed will grow in the near future. By the end of the 1980's only 80 percent of the labor force in an industrial plant will be full-time. By the mid-1990's this could be less than 50 percent. One form of part-time work is temporary employment. The majority of current "Temps," or temporary workers, however, hold low level jobs. Companies are unwilling or unable to continually train new people in the skills required for better positions. "Temps" generally receive a lower wage than full-time workers in the same job. They also are frequently ineligible for fringe benefits, are the last hired and the first fired when the economy slumps, and enjoy little control over their work environment.[16]

In the future this situation will probably change. As a result of the increasing levels of education required to function efficiently in the modern workplace, '"consultants" will replace "temps." Consultants will be highly trained specialists brought together for a specific project. Once the project is completed, the specialists will disband, eventually joining a new project. In this way employees will gain greater control over allocation of their time. Payment for project work will provide the necessary "plenty." Between projects the consultants will use this "plenty" to pursue other ideals according to their own desires and schedule.

Job sharing, a distant relative to temporary employment, is more efficient in terms of utilizing employee expertise to achieve corporate objectives. Robert Gilman's definition of job sharing is:

> . . . a formal, intentional arrangement that permits more than one person to hold, on a part time basis, a job in the cash economy which is full time. It is a remarkably flexible concept in terms of the time cycle of the sharing, the number of people per full time position, and the types of occupation to which it is applicable. The time sharing can range from division of a day to a change every several years.[17]

Nor is job sharing limited to a number of people filling one fulltime job. A number of jobs can be involved. Three people, for example, can fill two jobs.

One thing the "odd" partner or partners in a job sharing situation could become move involved in is community development. Such efforts would obviously benefit the company as well as the individual. A growing number of companies, in fact, have begun sponsoring employee service type activities in the contextual environment. Since the upheaval of the 1960's the amount of volunteer work carried on by U.S. employees has increased dramatically. As Norman Barnes says in his 1974 *Fortune* magazine article "Rethinking Corporate Charity":

> Beginning in the mid-'60's and spurred powerfully by the sight of American cities in flames, a fair number of senior executives became persuaded that business has both a moral obligation and a compelling need to deal with social problems—that just making money wasn't enough.[18]

Types of current employee volunteer work include:

1) Release Time-Employees receive time off, with pay, to volunteer for community service activities, usually on an hourly or daily basis.
2) Social Service Leave -Employees are given extended periods of time off from normal duties, sometimes several years, during which to carry out a community service.
3) Loaned Personnel- Employees with specific skills are assigned to help run a community organization, such as a school or charity, on an ongoing basis.
4) Group Project-The company itself organizes and carries out a community project, such as a fundraiser, using company employees exclusively.[19]

Some of the more advanced corporations have meshed departments assigned the duty of dealing with contextual environment problems directly into their organizational structure. The American Telephone and telegraph Company, for example, recently set up a Department of

Environmental Affairs to study and define approaches to such problems as water pollution and the fostering of experimental preschool learning programs in urban ghettos.[20] The above approaches differ from the job-sharing arrangement I described in that they are not a fully integrated facet of the total corporate operation. The involved pursuits are not included in employees job descriptions. Such programs, however, show the business sector's growing desire to break down boundaries between its internal and contextual environments, to close the gap between work and leisure time activities, and to improve the overall quality of life for employees as well as other stakeholders.

For job sharing and similar systems to work, however, major changes will obviously have to occur. Primarily, the private sector will have to generate enough wealth to support the new technology as well as the work force. This can be accomplished in two ways: 1) machines can increase production efficiency, therefore generating more financial profits to be divided among stakeholders; and 2) employees can accept additional free time, educational opportunities and other benefits in lieu of constantly increasing financial rewards.

In reality, alternative (1) is occurring and alternative (2) is beginning to occur. In order for the full potential of alternative (2) to be realized, however, socio-economic thinking must continue to evolve in its current direction.

Also, for this system to work organizational design must go through a radical transformation. This next challenge will be discussed in Chapter Seven.

SUMMARY

Unless the predicted changes in socio-economic thinking occur, we might eventually see economic and social upheaval during the post-lndustrial Revolution era. If emphasis reverts to the sole pursuit of plenty, those controlling the new technology will prosper while the masses lose control of their lives. One of the current trends making such a reversion improbable is in education. The new technology requires increasing levels of education as well as the continuous reeducation of employees. While necessitating such change, the new technology is also facilitating it. Computers, word processors, video equipment, and closed circuit TV are among the tools helping make quality education more generally available. They are allowing companies to develop innovative, inexpensive programs on their own and in partnership with the academic community. They are helping to erase the old educational constraints of time, place, and technique.

Increased educational opportunity is, in turn, encouraging employees to better define and organize personal development in terms of the pursuit of all four ideals. Employee's are again seeking emotional security, this time, however, to complement rather than to make up for their lack of physical security as in the Medieval Period. Surveys show that after a certain level of "plenty" is achieved, they are asking for more free time rather than further pay increases.

This shift of emphasis might offer a partial solution for the problem of unemployment produced by the new technology. Future employees will not put in as many hours. Because of the simultaneous increased efficiency of technology, jobs will be able to support more than one worker. Employees will function either as consultants, working on a project-by-project basis, or as part of a job-sharing team. The latter situation will encourage increased participation in the solution of contextual environment problems. Many companies are already sponsoring such involvement, though efforts, at this point, are still relatively unsophisticated.

Traditional forms of organizational design will no longer be functional if the above defined changes in workstyle occur. They are too restrictive in terms of their ability to adapt to increasing degrees of employee freedom. New forms must evolve. The possible nature of these new forms will be part of my discussion in Chapter Seven.

NOTES

1. Eli Ginzberg, "The Mechanization of Work," *Scientific American*, September 1982, p. 69.

2. Edward Reisner, *The Evolution of the Common School (New* York: Macmillan, 1930), p. 267.

3. Carol Hymowitz, "Employers Take Over Where Schools Fail to Teach the Basics," *Wall Street Journal*, January 22, 1981, p. 1.

4. Kenneth Huddleston and Dorothy Fenwick, "The Productivity Challenge: Business/Education Partnership," *Training and Development Journal*, Vol. 37, No. 4, April 1983, p. 97.

5. Fred Emery, *Futures We Are In* (Leiden, Sweden: Martinus Nijhoff Social Science Division, 1977), pp. 135-36.

6. Hymowitz, p. 22.

7. Huddleston and Fenwick, p. 98.

8. Ibid.

9. "Company Courses Go Collegiate," *Business Week*, February 26, 1979, p. 90

10. Ginzberg, p. 74.

11. David Jenkins, *Job Power* (Baltimore: Penguin Books, 1973), p. 39.

12. Wassily Leontief, "The Distribution of Work and Income," *Scientific American*, September 1982, p. 192.

13. Leontief, p. 195.

14. "New Breed of Workers," *U.S. News and World Report*, September 3, 1979, p. 36.

15. David Clutterbuck, "The Future of Work," *International Management*, August 1979, p. 18.

16. Thomas Brom, "The Parttime Job: A New Way of Life," *Philadelphia Bulletin*, December 3, 1978, p. 6.

17. Robert Gilman, "Job Sharing Is Good," *The Co-Evolutionary Quarterly*, Spring 1978, p. 86.

18. Norman Barnes, "Rethinking Corporate Charity," *Fortune Magazine,* October 1974, p. 168.

19. Kerry Allen, Isolda Chaplin, Shirley Keller, and Donna Hill *Volunteers from the Workplace,* National Center of Voluntary Action, Washington, D.C., 1979, p. 242.

20. Alvin Toffler *Future Shock* (New York: Random House, 1970), p. 454.

7

A Glimpse Into the Future of Management Theory

ORGANIZATION SIZE/DESIGN AS THE KEY ISSUE

Modern companies that wish to flourish must be capable of adapting to an accelerating rate of environmental change. For example, products and services are becoming obsolete with increasing rapidity. As economist Robert Theobald says, "Products that used to sell for twenty-five years now often count on no more than five. In the volatile pharmaceutical and electronics fields the period is often as short as six months."[1]

Companies still create trends, but individual firms can no longer dominate the scene. The competition in most profitable sectors is too fierce. The successful company, therefore, is the one capable of modifying its research and production capabilities quickly enough to satisfy a rapidly shifting variety of customer needs and desires.

The hierarchical structure, as we have traditionally known

it, does not provide the required degree of organizational flexibility. As Alvin Toffler says, the typical bureaucratic arrangement is "ideally suited to solving routine problems at a moderate pace. But when things speed up, or the problems cease to be routine, chaos often breaks loose."[2]

The office/shop of large, centralized operations has traditionally offered: 1) a home for an organization; 2) a place for people to come together face to face; 3) a work environment away from home; 4) a place to house centralized forms of manufacturing/communication technology too expensive for the home; and 5) a structured schedule.[3]

All this will change as the environment becomes increasingly turbulent. In the future the "organizational home" will often become a far-flung and shifting network of sites depending on the location of key individuals, rather than one building or group of buildings. This network will be tied together by sophisticated communication technology including video screens that allow "face to face" discussions without actual physical proximity. Because the employee will probably carry this equipment in his briefcase, the "work environment away from home" can be a hotel room, a resort, a boat, or someone else's house. According to Guiliano, the job will "no longer be tied to the flow of papers across a designated desk; it will, instead, be tied to the worker himself."[4] Employees, therefore, will "structure their own schedule" instead of depending on the company to do it.

The above described, extremely flexible network of employees will still, however require coordination and control mechanisms. An organizational model must be defined that couples freedom and authority with "bottom line" responsibilities. Models more sophisticated than Likert's are evolving. One of the most advanced, which is being developed by INTERACT's Jamshid Gharajedaghi, founder of the Inter-

101

national Management Institute of Iran, incorporates the above defined organizational characteristics. Gharajedaghi talks about a "Multilevel, Multidimensional, Modular-Organization."⁵ Six dimensions exist in the organization:

1) Output Units- These are autonomous product units responsible for manufacturing and distributing the item(s) or service(s) produced. These units are as self-sufficient as possible while maintaining the integrity of the organization as a whole. Personnel decide which production-related services to provide for themselves, which to purchase from external sources. While output units receive a share of their profits, as defined by the organization's planning/decision making unit, they must also accept part of annual losses.

2) Input Units-These units sell production-related services to output units which the latter are incapable of developing themselves. Input units are also as self-sufficient as possible. They can develop clients outside the company as long as no conflict of interest exists. At the same time, however, output units are not required to purchase production-related services from them. An outside competitor can be used if a better deal is found.

3) Environmental Unit—This unit helps the organization define its relationship with the external environment in terms of marketing, advocacy, employee education, and employee community project activity. It helps facilitate and coordinate research in these areas, selling skills and information to other units which the latter are incapable of generating themselves and cannot buy cheaper elsewhere. The environmental unit is as self-sufficient as possible. It seeks funding for employee projects from external as well as internal sources.

4) Planning/Decision Making Unit-Representatives from all organizational units sit on the planning/decision making unit board. They define the corporate mission and objectives, regulate and coordinate the activities of all organizational units, and deal with decision making at the corporate level.

5) Control Unit-Personnel in this unit are responsible for monitoring corporate achievement of its mission and objectives as defined by the planning unit. Control unit staff report only to the managing director.

6) Management Unit-The managing director and his staff are responsible for facilitating activities in the planning/decision making unit.

Each output unit is a replica of the organization as a whole. It contains output element subunits, input subunits, an environmental subunit, a control subunit, and a management subunit. Representatives from all these subunits sit on the board of the planning/decision making subunit.

Where appropriate, input units are also replicas of the organization as a whole.

The environmental unit is a replica of the organization as a whole except that it does not have environmental subunit. Its output subunits provide research and consulting services on markets, public opinion, educational opportunities, and community projects. It sells these services to other units that are unwilling or unable to develop them and which cannot purchase them more cheaply elsewhere.

The planning/decision making unit has new project subunits. These are controlled by the board until they become self-sufficient financially. It also has input subunits that provide specialized services to the new project subunits not offered by the organization's input units.

New project subunits can be financed by output units, input units, and the environmental unit. This support can take the form of stock shares purchased or direct loans. Once the new project subunit becomes self-sufficient such loans plus the accrued interest must be paid off.

If the new project subunits do not become self-sufficient within an acceptable period of time, profit-motivated "investors" will either supervise a reorganization or withdraw their support, causing the subunit to fail unless it can develop alternative sources of' financial support.

The output element subunits and service element subunits can have sub-subunits, and so on depending on organizational size and product sophistication.

A set percentage of profits is absorbed from each input, output, and environmental unit by the corporation. This "tax" as Gharajedaghi calls it, is defined by the planning/decision making board. Part of the revenues received are used to support the management and control units. The board can decide to loan another part to output, input, or environmental units interested in expanding their operation or experiencing financial difficulties. Units can also borrow from other units or from outside sources, but, in the latter case, only if the corporate level planning/decision making board approves. "Tax" revenues left over at year's end are carried over.

In terms of management, the benefits of this organizational design include the following:

1) Because output, input, and environmental units are profit centers and because all employees share in profits/losses according to a formula defined by the corporate level planning/decision making board, emphasis is on operational efficiency. As a result bureaucracy will be cut to a

minimum, and, therefore, will be less of' an impediment to the management process.

2) All employees will have direct access to the planning/decision making board at their own level and indirect access to planning/decision making boards at higher levels through their representatives on those boards.

3) Because planning/decision making is a continuous process involving all levels which allows frequent comparisons of actual versus expected outcomes, the design facilitates learning and adaptation.

4) Due to the closely knit network of planning/decision making boards, organizational and unit objectives are continuously reviewed and kept in close alignment.

MARKETPLACE PRESSURES AS THE KEY ISSUE

If the cyclical nature of the evolutionary process being defined remains on course, once organizational size/design is modernized, marketplace pressures will emerge as the focal issue. The emphasis in socio-economic doctrine will increasingly have swung away from the exclusive pursuit of "plenty" toward a more balanced quest for all four ideals. As this "swing" occurs, shoppers will begin buying for different reasons. While the quest for "plenty" dominates, status is determined largely by the quantity and quality of goods and services a person can display. Someone who drives a Cadillac is better respected than someone who can afford only a bicycle. The person who dresses in a blouse bearing a popular designer's emblem is more attractive than one who continues to wear last year's plain tee-shirt, no matter how clean he keeps it. Expensive restaurants provide a name to drop as well as good food. Charles Reich claims in *The Greening of*

America that such doctrinal narrowness causes a "loss of self." He says that "beginning with school, if not before, an individual is systematically stripped of his imagination, his creativity, his heritage, his dreams, and his personal uniqueness in order to style him into a production (and consumption) unit for mass technology society."[6] To replace the "lost self" such individuals are given by the advertising world "status" defined largely in terms of the degree of plenty achieved.

The attendant conflict ethic reinforces this emphasis on material possessions and the ability to purchase the services/attendance of others. Because conflict is defined in win-lose terms, the need is to find ways to prove oneself superior. This is done by sporting a wider selection of expensive shoes than anyone else, by being the first kid on your block to display the latest electronic gadget, by treating waiters/waitresses and other service personnel condescendingly.

Then, at the age of forty or so, many a successful disciple goes through an "identity crisis." He or she has a good job, an abundance of plenty, a respectable degree of status and number of "wins." But something important is missing. That "something," of course, is a true sense of "self" in all its dimensions. Physical security, unfortunately, has been confused with emotional security. Instead of functioning as part of an inseparable, interdependent combination, the former has been thought to encompass the latter.

With the current shift in doctrine, however, this attitude is changing. People are turning more to the ideals of truth, good, and beauty as sources of emotional security and identity. Status is being defined increasingly in terms of content, rather than image. Put another way, people are once again becoming more interested in what they can *do* than in which they can buy. For example, future status will come from understanding and being able to share what is in the *Harvard*

Classics, rather than from owning the most expensive set. Status will come from taking the time to learn how to paint or to truly understand what motivated the impressionists, rather than simply from owning a Van Gogh original. Status will come from being able to explain the workings of an automobile engine, rather than from simply owning an expensive car. People are realizing gradually 1) that the process through which one achieves content is the essence of human development; 2) that content cannot be bought, it must be carefully cultivated: 3) that only image can be bought; and 4) that image alone has very little to do with wholistic human and societal development.

In terms of marketplace pressures, then, consumers are beginning to purchase goods and services for different reasons. Because nonmaterial pursuits are increasingly important, plenty is becoming less an end in itself. Rather, it is becoming the means for fulfilling a better balanced spectrum of needs and desires. As a result, corporate profits will depend more on enhancing a product or service's attractiveness in terms of usefulness than on simply developing and pushing an ever-growing array of "impression pieces." What an item looks like, the label it carries will seem less critical than its effectiveness in meeting a functional need, than its power to enable customers to do or learn something as individuals.

AND FINALLY, SOCIO-ECONOMIC DOC-TRINE AS THE KEY ISSUE

In a future resulting from the trends I have discussed, the dominant organizational ethic in the internal and contextual environments will change radically. In the internal environment a cooperative/competitive ethic will increasingly replace the conflict ethic. For example, members of a job sharing team will cooperate while job sharing teams compete. In the contextual environment competition refereed by the government will define interaction between companies struggling for marketplace shares while a cooperative ethic will guide joint corporate efforts to solve social and environmental problems.

Conflict with its win-lose approach will no longer be an acceptable alternative. Inefficiency in terms of both human and nonhuman resources will eventually cause its demise. People in a cooperative or well-designed competitive situation expend a majority of their physical, intellectual, and emotional energies in pursuit of positive goals. By this I mean goals that enhance one or more facets of their development. In a conflict situation a vast amount of physical, intellectual, and emotional energy is expended either in constructing defense mechanisms or in attempting to hinder the opposition's development.

In some respects, conflict should be called a "lose-lose" instead of a "win-lose" situation. Very rarely does a "winner" not lose something of value along the way, be it physical or emotional. Especially in our modern world of increasingly interdependent systems, such "losses" seem impossible to avoid. This might be one of the reasons that, as Barry Commoner says in his book *The Closing Circle*, "Everywhere in the world there is evidence of a deep-seated failure in the effort to use the competence, the wealth, the power at human disposal for the maximum good of human beings."[7] Nonhuman resources, such as time, are wasted in unproductive defense building pursuits or in semi-productive to unproductive acts of aggression. They are also squandered/ destroyed by people so intent on winning the battle that they lose the war for everyone including themselves. Conflict situations, because of the constant threat and paranoia involved, tend to make contestants short-sighted. The tragic toxic waste problem faced by the United States today is an example of such short-sightedness. In order to "win," company and government officials have been willing to abdicate their social responsibility .

If western society is to thrive, and perhaps survive, it can no longer afford to squander such a large portion of its human and nonhuman resources on nondevelopmental and antidevelopmental pursuits. Commoner gives the following opinion concerning the destruction of nonhuman resources.

> My own judgement, based on the evidence now at hand, is that the present course of environmental degradation, at least in industrialized countries, represents a challenge to essential ecological systems so serious that, if continued, it will destroy the capability of the environment to support a reasonably civilized human society.... One can try to guess at the point of no return—the time at which major ecological degradation might be irreparable. In my own judgement, a reasonable estimate for industrialized areas of the world might be from twenty to fifty years, but it is only a guess.[8]

THE CHANGING ROLES OF KEY STAKEHOLDERS

The roles of key stakeholders in the contextual environment will also change. Traditionally, industry has exploited resources found there. With notable exceptions it has, at the same time, refused to take responsibility for the physical and social damage done. The role of government has been to force industry, indirectly, to pay for its exploitation privileges, using monies collected through taxation to repair environmental damage and to deal with social problems such as unemployment. The public's role has been to exert pressure on the government to pass and enforce laws protecting consumers and inhabitants of the environment exploited by industry. Counter-pressures to limit governmental constraints have, of course, been exerted by citizens and stockholders profiting greatly from industrial practices. Post-Industrial Revolution influences will modify these roles. The logic of my argument is as follows. Microprocessors will be used whenever possible to increase productivity. This shift will be necessary if western society is to remain competitive in the world market. Because of the increased efficiency of computer technology a growing number of jobs will be automated in the two still sizable economic sectors- manufacturing and services. As Eric Trist says,

> This family of [microprocessor run] technologies has applications in all industries, whether manufacturing or service. It is a universal with consequences which are pervasive.... Mass unemployment is likely unless offsetting measures are drawn up in advance.[9]

The welfare system, at least as we now know it in western

110

society, will not support the predicted number of unemployed. Those still able to pay taxes will balk at the increased rates. Recipients, on the other hand, because of shifts in socioeconomic doctrine and the accompanying rise in educational levels will find the quality of life made possible unacceptable. Two alternatives exist in this situation: 1) the use of force to keep stakeholders from attempting to change the system; and 2) reorganization of the system to make it acceptable both to supporters and recipients.

In modern, industrialized democratic/socialistic societies alternative number one is unlikely. If alternative number two is chosen, major changes will have to be made. Again, two approaches are possible: 1) government can attempt to design and run this new, more sophisticated social service system; and 2) the private sector can design and manage the system.

Some governments have already attempted to develop a workable apparatus for instituting an acceptable reapportionment. Most of the involved nations are currently in deep financial trouble.

Claims are that their social welfare programs have created unacceptable governmental growth and that the expense of big government is ruining economies. President Reagan in his 1981 inaugural address said that, "In the present [economic] crisis government is not the solution to our problem. Government is the problem."[10] In 1982 Fritz Leutweiler, head of the Swiss National Bank, said simply, "the public sector has been permitted to grow too large."[11] According to Wharton Econometrics Forecasting Associates data, the percentage of the gross domestic product expended for welfare benefits by a majority of the western industrialized countries had doubled or nearly doubled since 1960. In Sweden it has jumped from 27 percent to 63 percent, in Denmark from 21 percent to 57 percent, in Italy from 20 percent to 51 percent, in Germany from 28 percent to 43 percent, in France from 26 percent to 48 percent, in the United Kingdom from 29 percent to 43 percent, and in the United States from 27 percent to 30 percent.[12] J. A. Livingstone, an economics correspondent for the *Philadelphia Inquirer*, explains, the overall situation in terms of the United States. He says that if government deficits here are not reduced, either by raising taxes or curtailing expenditures, the nation faces a "decade or more of dangerously inadequate investment in production plant equipment, research, development, and public infrastructure. This we fear is a prescription for economic stagnation with no end in sight."[13]

THE PRIVATE SECTOR TAKES OVER

It is interesting to me that a majority of private and public sector critics, when addressing the problem, see one major cure as a cutback in the number of social services delivered. Such cutbacks, for example, are already occurring in the U.S. educational and health care sectors. Very few critics talk about a need to increase the efficiency of the involved systems, to find ways to deliver more services for less cost. Perhaps they consider such reasoning useless. Governmental bureaucracies are traditionally less productive than those found in the private sector. They are larger and more rigid. Because of the lack of a profit motive, little efficiency-encouraging incentive exists. Very rarely do employees improve their salaries by being innovative. More likely, such acts endanger their job security by threatening superiors. Promotions are based more on tenure and "getting along" rather than on improved performance. The system, in fact, actually encourages inefficiency. Prestige and salary are frequently based on the number of employees under one's control.

Emphasis, therefore, is on adding to one's staff, rather than on doing the job as cheaply and with as few people as possible. Corruption is also encouraged by this arrangement. Most employees cannot increase their share of plenty rapidly by doing a good job Some can, however, do so by making deals with contractors. Organizational "profits" do not suffer from their misdeeds, so associates have less incentive to expose such practices. Also, because of the size of most operations, accurate control measures are difficult to institute.

The obvious alternative to changing governmental performance is to take the involved responsibility away, not simply by shifting it to other levels as President Reagan has proposed, but entirely. Efficiency is a cornerstone of the private sector. This efficiency has been used to conquer a multitude of internal technical and social system problems. It can be used to do the same with similar problems in the contextual environment. As Hasan Ozbekhan says, "We hear increasingly that it is the responsibility of business to take the lead in 'environmental creation'; that it would be against our tradition to let government do this; that business has the planning, management, and technical know-how to put the environment back 'on its feet, in a businesslike way."[14]

Both the contextual environment and business would profit. In terms of the environment, Archie Boe, Chairman of Allstate Insurance Company, says:

> ... A cash contribution to this charity or that can no longer suffice to meet the needs that society brings to our door. Corporations must now exert their influence to encourage their people to become personally involved in working out solutions to the major social and economic problems facing our society today.[15]

In terms of the business community, the Committee for Economic Development released the following statement:

> It is the "enlightened self-interest" of corporations to promote the public welfare in a positive way.... People who have a good environment, education, and opportunity make better employees, customers, and neighbors for business than those who are poor, ignorant and oppressed.[16]

One immediate savings would be in cutting out the middleman. Instead of paying the government to provide services, industry would provide them directly, using its ingenuity to constantly improve both the efficiency of the delivery system and the effectiveness of the service delivered

Government's role would be to establish appropriate incentives. These incentives might take the form of tax breaks rather than contracts. Tax breaks can be delivered after the fact, thus insuring performance and guarding against overruns. The government would also set standards and monitor efforts.

Such an arrangement would require a tremendous amount of planning, coordination, and cooperation. The traditional win-lose mode of interaction between the private and public sectors would no longer be functional. The shift to a cooperative ethic would be facilitated by government's shrinking and less expensive role. It would also be facilitated by business's currently increasing sense of social and environmental responsibility. Emphasis, in many cases, would shift from problem solution to problem prevention. Rather than simply paying displaced workers unemployment benefits, companies would, for example, support them while they used their experience and expertise to define novel ways to bring in additional profits. New private sector jobs would also materialize with the undertaking of social sector projects. These jobs, if part of a sharing system, would allow employees to enjoy increased diversity in their working lives. The corporate world, therefore, would stand to gain more than it lost by adopting the "new" cooperation-based doctrine. Sandra Holmes, in her study of top corporate executive attitudes toward social responsibility, asked participants to identify benefits they thought likely to result from such involvement. Her results included the following:

1) 97.4 percent believed that corporate reputation and goodwill would be enhanced;
2) 89 percent believed that the social system in which the corporation functioned would be strengthened;
3) 74.3 percent believed that the economic system in which the corporation functioned would be strengthened;
4) 72.3 percent pointed to greater job satisfaction among all employees, and 62.8 percent to greater job satisfaction among executives;
5) 63.7 percent believed that additional governmental regulation would be avoided;
6) 60.7 percent believed that the firm's chances of survival would improve;
7) 55.5 percent believed that the ability to attract better managerial talent would result;
8) 52.9 percent believed that long-run profitability would increase. [17]

I would add that such a movement, if well organized and large scale, should also provide: 1) a means for decreasing taxes while at the same time creating new jobs; and 2) a way of improving the esthetic dimension of worklife for all employees through their own efforts.

THE VISION FADES

This is where I must stop. If the predicted changes in organizational size/design, marketplace pressures, and socio-economic thinking do actually occur during the next 20, 50, or 100 years, technology should eventually emerge again as the key issue. I have no idea, however, of the nature of such a futuristic technology. My only suggestion is that whatever it is, it will complement the predicted changes in socio-economic thinking.

In a way, my ending has taken us back to the beginning, and, therefore, is a new beginning. The new beginning, however, is much richer than the old one. Whereas during the Medieval period emphasis was on emotional security because the problems of physical security had not yet been solved, in the future emphasis will shift again to emotional security, but this time because the problems of physical security have been solved.

In terms of ethics, the emphasis on cooperation during the Medieval period was forced, at least partially, by uncontrollable environmental circumstances. People had no alternative. They had to cooperate in order to survive. Modern cooperation will be the product of the realization that it is the most effective means of facilitating both individual and organization development.

The cult of individualism did not surface during the Medieval period because the means necessary to achievement of individual preeminence were not generally obtainable. Such means, in terms of plenty at least, became available to increasing numbers of seekers during the Renaissance, the Reformation, and the Industrial Revolution. Today, almost everyone in technologically advanced societies has access to them. Because everyone has access, however, uniqueness is again difficult to achieve. Also, because of the increased amounts of plenty available and the resultant switch to the pursuit of other ideals, the conflict ethic which spawned individualism is being replaced by a cooperative ethic which encourages "teamism."

Emphasis during the Medieval period was on what people could do, rather than what they had. This was the result of current socio-economic thinking doctrine and an initial shortage of the ingredients of physical security. Today, we are again becoming more interested in what we can do. This latest shift, however, has occurred, not because of shortages, but as a result of the realization that human development is a product of "content" rather than "image."

And finally, due largely to their size, medieval businesses were worker oriented. They had little need for bureaucracies and fewer hierarchical levels. They were structured so that all craftsmen could contribute to the problem solving process. Today we are again trying to do away with the inefficient aspects of bureaucracies and hierarchies. We are attempting to design organizations that will allow output, input, environmental planning, control, and management units as well as the organization as a whole to best utilize the expertise of unit employees.

NOTES

1. Eric Toffler, *Future Shock* (New York: Random House, 1970), p. 72.

2. Toffler, p. 139.

3. Vincent Guiliano, "The Mechanization of Office Work," *Scientific American*, September 1982, p. 163.

4. Ibid.

5. Jamshid Gharajedaghi, "Organizational Implications of Systems Thinking: Multidimensional Modular *Design*," *European Journal of Operations Research*, August 1984.

6. Charles Reich, *(The Greening of America* (New York: Random House 1970), p.18.

7. Barry Commoner, *'The Closing Circle "* New York: Alfred A. Knopf, 1971), p.294.

8. Ibid., pp. 217, 232.

9. Eric Trist, "The Evolution of Socio-Technical Systems," Issues in the Quality of Working Life, No. 2. Ontario: Ministry of Labor, 1980, p. 50.

10. A. J. Livingston, "The 80s: The Dangerous Decade," *Philadelphia Inquirer*, February 28, 1983, 9-C.

11. Ibid.

12. Livingston, February 27, 1983, 2-F.

13. Livingston, March 3, 1983, 17-C.

14. Hasan Ozbekhan, "Toward a General Theory of Planning," University of Pennsylvania, 1982.

15. Kerry Allen, Isolda Chaplin, Shirley Keller, and Donna Hill, *Volunteers from The Workplace,* National Center of Voluntary Action, Washington, D.C., 1979, p.iv.

16. Ibid., p. 9.

17. Ibid., p. 8.

8

Getting There From Here

Obstacles To Change

We are developing a pretty good idea of where we want to
go in terms of social doctrine and management practices. The
question is, "How do we get there?" During the Reformation,
when the transition was toward individualism, conflict, and
increased physical security at the expense of togetherness and
emotional security, the vehicle was a convenient interpretation of the beliefs of Luther and Calvin. As decades passed,
continued movement in this direction was supported by the
economic theories of Adam Smith, Thomas Malthus, William
Graham Sumner, and Herbert Spenser. Even today we have
those who advocate the same "law of the jungle" approach to
economic and human development, though their audience is
shrinking.

Evidence of the survival of this mindset in the business
sector is provided by the U.S.'s modern day robber barons who
are probably less ethical than their predecessors. The Carnegies,
Rockefellers, Vanderbilts and Morgans of an earlier era build
key pieces of our economic infrastructure while amassing their
personal fortunes. Today's version, the leverage buyout artists, the Wall Street scam artists, however, are doing so at the
expense of that infrastructure. While the original robber barons were guided at least partially by religious convictions and
used part of their wealth to create colleges and other society-

improving institutions, today's version seems to be guided solely by greed and to feel no responsibility for the damage done to individual employees, financially gutted firms, and society in general.

Emphasis On The Quantitative

We also have a very strong school of modern day scientific advocates, those whose aim is to quantify as many facets - human as well as technical — of a business as possible. These advocates have found a powerful ally in the computer. For one thing, the computer has made previously discussed robotics, the answer to Frederick Taylor's wildest dreams, possible. While Taylor's attempts to turn workers into machines, to define how many pieces of coal a shoveler should pick up with each scoop, how far he should bend his knees and back each time, how fast he should walk while carrying the coal to the furnace, in order to maximize productivity made sense theoretically, actual implimentation presented insurmountable problems. Employees refused to cooperate. They had little desire to be turned into machines.

As a result of this "attitude problem," while Taylor's approach survived in textbooks under the heading of "scientific management" (which is a serious and even dangerous misnomer due to the one-directional light it puts science in) it rarely survived on the shop or office floor. Now, however, employee-replacing robots are, indeed, a piece of the mechanical process and can be programmed to go through their paces without variation.

A second modern day happening supporting the mechanistic perspective which had been aided by the advent of the computer is the development of the science of operations research (OR). OR was borne in the 1930s as an interdisciplinary approach to management problems. This approach, again, was quantitative. The complementary capabilities of the computer allowed OR practitioners to model complex systems containing large numbers of variables. More specifically according to Stafford Beer and the Operations Research Society of Great Britain:

"Operations research is the attack of modern science on complex problems arising in the direction and management of large systems of men, machines, materials and money in industry, business, government and defense. Its distinctive approach is to develop a scientific model of the system, incorporating measurements of factors such as change and risk, with which to predict and compare the outcomes of alternative decisions, strategies or controls. The purpose is to help management determine its policy and actions scientifically. [1]"

The first U.S. degree program in OR was started in 1952 at Case Institute of Technology by Russell Ackoff. During this period the management training sector of academia, in general, began placing increasing emphasis on the development of quantitative, as opposed to people, skills. This shift was supported by the Carnegie Institute and the Rockefeller Institute Reports which appeared in the late 50s and stated in essence that there was too much fluff in management sciences and management education, especially at the graduate level, that they had to become more scientifically rigorous if they were going to prepare students to function effectively in the modern day workplace.

Integration of the Quantitative and the Non-quantitative

During these same years, however, a counter trend also appeared. It was becoming increasingly obvious to Ackoff and a growing number of other quantitative-oriented, or "hard" scientists that, while modeling worked well in defining the flow of technical systems and material goods, problems arose when attempts were made to incorporate social variables, or

121

the human side of operations. Employees actions were less easily defined, less predictable, and more difficult to quantify than those of machines. Also, being "purposeful" rather than "purposive" systems, employees had their own agendas, needs and wants, just as important to them as those of the organization, which affected performance. These personal variables were constantly changing in unpredictable ways and were almost impossible to effectively factor into OR models, but tended to significantly impact process results.

The humanists, in the meantime, were not asleep. They had not given up in their battle with the "hard" sciences which had now raged for most of the century. Psychologists and sociologists had joined the ranks of those focusing on the employee rather than the machine in attempts to increase output. Organizations such as The Tavistock Institute in England and the University of Michigan's Institute for Social Research became increasingly active. The QWL movement began producing landmark studies like the one at the Western Electric Company's Hawthorne plant in Chicago which rediscovered and validated the fact that employees are more productive when you pay attention to them, when you get them involved and give them a chance to use and develop their potential, than when you don't.

Those battling on the humanist side, however, also eventually realized they couldn't do it alone. Processes on all levels of businesses were becoming increasingly sophisticated. To believe that employee motivation alone could produce the desired results was unrealistic. An either-or approach was no longer reasonable. Some way had to be found to marry the mechanistic/quantitative school and the humanistic/qualitative school, and to generate a new perspective which was comprehensive and which complemented the new socio-economic doctrine that was evolving.

Enter The Systems Approach

The vehicle chosen for developing this new way of viewing management was the "systems approach," which sprang originally from the work of Ludwig Von Bertalanffy and was laid out in his book, **General Systems Theory: Foundations, Development, Applications**, published in 1968. The systems approach was developed originally in the 1920s and 30s to provide a new perspective for the life sciences, specifically organismic biology. Rapidly, however, through the work of Von Bertalanffy, Kenneth Boulding, Anatol Rapoport, R. W. Gerard and a growing number of others, its applicability to a wide range of other disciplines including mathematics, psychology, economics, communications theory, evolution theory, physiology, and education became obvious.

Basic components of the systems approach included the facts that:

1. It relies on "holism" as a methodology - The primary technique used in scientific investigation since the time of Galileo and Newton has been analysis. Break things down to their smallest component parts. Define the role of these parts. Then combine your definitions to gain an understanding of the whole. Von Bertalanffy pointed out that systems of all types must be explored not only in terms of their components, but also in terms of the full range of relationships existing between these components if one is to gain a true understanding of how they function. This is necessary in part because systemic wholes possess characteristics which none of their parts possess and which greatly impact performance. When one analyzes, breaks down, these is no way to identify these characteristics of the whole.

123

2. It provides a means of breaking down the traditional boundries in both the philosophical and scientific realms and between these realms — When one works to understand a systemic whole, the environment containing that system must be studied as well as its parts and their interactions. The economic systems of a society, for example, cannot be successfully understood without developing an appropriate understanding of that society's communications and education systems. Especially with social, or "socio," as opposed to technical systems, the environment greatly affects the way they function. This outward as well as inward view necessarily involves other disciplines.

3. It provides a means of making individual and societal development the most critical measure of scientific progress— The wholistic nature of the systems approach forces practitioners to address the "why?" as well as the "what?" and "how?" questions. When we discuss a system's relationship to its environment we must now ask more than, "What are its component parts?" and "How can we make it operate more efficiently?" We must begin by defining the role it plays and should play in that environment. What purpose does it serve? What benefits does or should it provide? Such a frame of reference is necessary so we can develop standards and make comparisons. Systems theory, therefore, chooses as its foundation the theory of human and societal development, and measures its progress in terms of that foundation.

Systems Theory in the Management Sector

By the mid and late 50s, the systems perspective began invading the realm of management theory as well. It was a good fit due to the previously mentioned growing realization in the business world that the split between the mechanistic/quantitative and the humanist/qualitative perspectives had to be mended. They were two sides of the same coin. The value of one could not be realized fully without also realizing the value of the other and understanding the involved interdependancies.

It was also a good fit due to the growing realization in the business world that workers were "purposeful" rather than "purposive" systems like machines. While the latter had one set of needs—electricity, maintenance, etc.— built into them by their designers, workers had two sets. The first included those necessary to the fulfilling of contractual obligations — periodic training in new technologies, periodic evaluations, word processing skills. The second included individual, private needs which were far more complex, and involved not only the immediate work environment, but also the home and community.

Traditional management was having trouble dealing effectively with workers focused increasingly on their individual rather than on their contractual needs. It was having trouble responding positively to the growing realization that work should no longer need to be an obligatory sacrifice of time, energy, and under-utilized potential required to gain the resources necessary to physical security and to the enjoyment of life during leisure hours; that work itself should provide the chance for the development of individual potential. It was having trouble, in essence, dealing with the new socio-economic thinking that was emerging.

A more comprehensive perspective was obviously necessary. Discussions concerning the nature of and the quest for human and societal development again sprang up in board room, staff, and union gatherings. The words spoken were still often drowned out by loud, adamant cries that the only important thing was to "Make more money!", to "Win!" to "Beat!" But the suspicion was growing that something very important was missing, and that systems theory might provided the answer.

The men who led the charge in the management sciences

125

sector included P. Selznick, Fred Emery, Eric Trist, and Russell Ackoff. In 1973 Dr. Ackoff, with degrees in architecture and philosophy; Dr. Trist, one of the founders of the Tavistock Institute whose training was in social psychology; Dr. Hasan Ozbekhan, one of the founders of the Club of Rome with degrees in economics, political science, and law; Dr. Tom Satty, a modern day leader in the field of mathematics; and Jim Emshoff, one of the rising stars in the field of Operations Research, formed the Social Systems Sciences Doctoral Program at The Wharton School of the University of Pennsylvania.

The program's purpose was to wed "hard" and "soft" management related sciences into a new paradigm that was systemic in nature. Students were accepted from all fields—operations research, social work, philosophy, psychology, fine arts, statistics, health care, mathematics, management. All were required to study philosophy initially, with emphasis on development theory, starting with the work of the ancient Greeks. They were then required to take a mix of "hard" courses, "soft" courses, and courses which melded the two.

The two interdependent vehicles developed by the Social Systems Sciences Department staff to introduce systems theory to the workplace were in the areas of strategic planning and organization design. "Interactive," or "proactive" planning as it came to be called, proposed a team effort involving everyone in the organization on a continual basis.

The paradigm grew from the realization that due to the increasing degree of turbulence found in the environment, the increasing difficulty in generating projections which remained accurate for the necessary length of time, organizations had to be restructured so that they were capable of learning from their environment on a continual basis and of adapting rapidly to what they learned. In order to "plan" effectively in this manner, therefore, management systems had to be structured in that way which took the greatest advantage of the eyes, ears, and expertise of all employees on all levels. More open communication channels had to be developed. Increased access to information had to be allowed. Problem solving and decision making procedures had to be modified.

In order to win employees over to this new culture, rather than having them feel threatened and fight it, the necessity grew for companies to become increasingly aware of individual employee needs. This brought up the issues of job security, rewards, and employee development. The end result, when such a planning and organization design paradigm was successfully introduced, had to be a more holistic, or systemic perspective.

A Passing Fad?

By the late 80's, the systems approach to management had been given fad status and dismissed by most. It had proven too radical. It had threatened too many people. In the still highly competitive work place, and especially in the U.S. where quantitative oriented executives preferred to treat employees as numbers and continued to see the best avenue to short-term improvement in the bottom line as a reduction in those numbers, people were loath to share information and problem solving/decision making responsibilities for fear of compromising their job security.

Also, it was hard to put boundaries around the systems approach, which turned out to be more a way of thinking than an exact science or collection of tools and techniques. It was difficult to define the expertise needed to be a systemic manager, and in a culture moving increasingly toward specialization and exact job descriptions, this was a disincentive.

Finally, systems thinking had developed a reputation for being too esoteric, for being mainly an academic exercise. Most of the critical writings coming out of the movement were extremely scholarly. They were almost impossible for the layman to make sense of, or to use effectively.

Academia, as well, was threatened. Professors in the management field had also become highly specialized. Little or no linkage existed between courses offered by quantitative and non-quantitative departments. Most MBA programs, as a result of the previously discussed drive to become "more scientifically rigorous," focused on quantitative skills — finance, statistics, production, macroeconomics, microeconomics, etc. Each of these subjects was taught as a stand-alone course, very little being done to integrate the involved learning. The non-quantitative parts of the degree program were often offered in an almost perfunctory manner. There was human resources, and some sort of course in group process skills. A lot of programs felt obliged to include a course or seminar on ethics, though no one was really sure of how best to teach the subject.

An attempt to pull this together into a comprehensive whole, to develop strong interdependencies and linkages was seen as a serious threat by many of the both quantitative and non-quantitative specialists whose turf was being invaded. It was seen as an attempt to dilute their offerings. Students would not learn enough to be truly effective in any specific skill area if the systems approach was accepted as the program's central theme.

Enter the Quality Improvement Movement

The new buzzword, at this point in history, had become "quality improvement." As we have said, the U.S. and Europe had begun losing world market share to Japan and other economic powers growing on the Pacific Rim. The U.S. was losing world market share also to European countries. One difference was quality. Following WWII, when everyone else was rebuilding and there was no real competition, the U.S. had been able to sell just about anything it produced. "Planned obsolescence" had become a popular concept during this period. Companies designed products so that they wouldn't last too long, thus increasing sales.

Customers didn't appreciate this approach, but were stuck with it until the rebuilt Japanese and European industrial sectors picked up on the quality theory. The U.S., suddenly, had to play catch-up in terms of management theory. Attention here focused initially on the duties of the Quality Control Manager, that person at the end of the line who was in charge of inspecting and rejecting defective parts before they got out the door. It rapidly became obvious, however, that in terms of the bottom line, this was not the most effective approach. Ways had to be found to keep defective widgets from being produced in the first place. The key was to encourage employees on all levels to take responsibility for quality and to make this responsibility a permanent part of their job. The best vehicle for facilitating such a change was the team.

Organizations also quickly realized that in order to gain the necessary level of commitment to the involved changes *from* employees, they had to start demonstrating a higher level of commitment *to* employees. Job security, equitable pay, improvements in the quality of the work environment, and opportunities for job related development became issues.

Members of successful quality improvement teams normally began by making improvements in those parts of the operation which most immediately affected them. In primary industry, for example, a large number of initial improvement projects had to do with safety.

Once the team's own "25 square feet" had been policed, members began addressing relationships with border functions. The team centered circles of interest continued to widen and overlap (remember Likert?) until they encompassed all organization systems from the smallest to the largest. By this time most stretched beyond the office or factory walls and parking lot. They addressed such issues as the lack of day care or elder care facilities, inadequate public transportation, poor schools, drugs, a poor regional image in terms of labor- management relations — issues which took on increasing importance once in-house systems had been put in order.

What was evolving was a participative, holistic, on-going process which, by its nature, had to eventually take into account the "Why?" questions, the developmental issues, and view these in terms of not only the organization and its employees, but also in terms of the larger environment of which the organization was a part—the community, region, country, or world—depending on size. What was evolving, if we view the quality improvement movement from a historical perspective, was, of course, a fleshed out version of the systems approach to management dressed in more comfortable, recognizable clothes and incorporating the wisdom of earlier pioneers from both the "hard" and the "soft" sides, the Taylors, Gilbreths, Gantts, Emersons, the Sheldons, Follets, Mayos, Herzbergs, Likerts.

Heading Dead On

At this point in history the quality improvement movement is still struggling through its formative states. There is a lot of confusion. A lot of companies are getting pieces of the puzzle in place. Too many, however, are learning the hard and often expensive lesson that one or two good pieces do not a successful whole make.

The quality movement, however, should eventually succeed, for it is not just another passing fad but the latest stop in an evolutionary progression which began at least five hundred years ago. It is the vehicle which gives us the power to make the changes in our socio-economic thinking that we have been talking about, the changes we have been sacrificing for, building up to for centuries. We might not get there today. We might back away again. But we are definitely drawing closer to that historic corner which, once we have turned it, will open the new world up to us, a world in which the development of positive individual and societal potential becomes our major objective.

SUMMARY OF BOOK

In this Book I have discussed the evolution of management theory in the workplace through the pre-Industrial Revolution, early Industrial Revolution, Middle Industrial Revolution, late Industrial Revolution, and post-Industrial Revolution eras, and on into the future. I have defined the influence of four key variables-socio-economic thinking, technological innovation, organizational size/design, and marketplace pressures—on this evolution. I have also attempted to show the relationship between management theory and human development, which involves the quest for both physical and emotional security.

The pre-Industrial Revolution era was divided into three periods, the Medieval period, the Renaissance, and the Reformation. During the Medieval period physical security was available to very few. Socio-economic doctrine, therefore, emphasized the cooperative ethic, service to God and community in return for spiritual rewards. Technology consisted mainly of hand powered tools. Businesses were small and run like families in which everyone contributed to decision making efforts. Markets were also small and local, with marketplace competition controlled by guilds.

During the Renaissance, due largely to progress in technical systems, profits, organizational size, and markets grew. The cooperative, family nature of businesses changed as the pursuit of wealth became possible for an increasing number. It was replaced by a conflict, win-lose ethic. The cult of individualism developed. Workers were no longer treated with the respect required by religion and social tradition.

131

This change in attitude was justified, in part, by the Protestant Ethic which evolved during the Reformation. Interpretations of this new religion excused, with the argument of "predestination," the exploitation, sometimes inhumane, of others. This convenient change in socio-economic thinking set the stage for the early Industrial Revolution. It was reinforced by the pronouncements of the classical economists who thought that the greatest good for the greatest number would be achieved by allowing individuals to pursue their own enlightened self-interest. New technology was the main issue during the early Industrial Revolution. A series of inventions allowed almost unlimited energy, standardization, and mass production. A small group of very powerful men controlled the marketplace. In this environment three organizational levels developed—the workers, frequently considered simply another machine part to be used in the most efficient manner until worn out, then to be discarded; middle management which was responsible for operational problem solving; and upper level management which made all the important decisions. This arrangement, however, contained the seeds of its own demise. By crowding large numbers of laborers into mining and manufacturing sites, management gave them the opportunity to compare notes and organize. Unions soon began demanding a larger share of the plenty made available by their efforts. The ensuing confrontation was often violent because of the still dominant conflict ethic, but an increasingly better educated labor force gradually gained power in political as well as economic arenas.

Eventually also, toward the end of this period, academia became involved in solving the problems of the workplace. Its emphasis was initially on helping management increase worker efficiency. The realization soon came, however, that labor's role must change if businesses were to thrive in the future.

Thus, during the middle part of the Industrial Revolution the human relations movement began. Its initial objective was to improve conditions for lower level employees. Organizational size/design also emerged as a focal issue. Businesses had traditionally been structured as hierarchies/ bureaucracies. As they grew larger this arrangement became increasingly inefficient. Academia especially began studying ways to break down the hierarchy and better utilize the growing employee expertise found on all levels. Most management teams, however, continued to ignore or to rationalize their situation. The hierarchy, despite its shortcomings, allowed them to maintain control of their environment, to insure their share of plenty and their individual superiority in the win-lose atmosphere engendered by current socioeconomic thinking.

It took increasing marketplace pressure during the late Industrial Revolution to force the issue. Societies that industrialized at a later date learned from the West's mistakes. Their businesses were organized with fewer levels. Incentive systems encouraged cooperation within organizations and government-regulated competition between organizations. Such companies began to take business away from less efficient European and U.S. sectors.

At the same time, socio-economic thinking was beginning to shift again in the western world. Workers were beginning to seek emotional security to accompany their growing share of physical security. Scholars and employees alike began attempting to define the important ingredients of human development. Systems scientists chose Greek thinking on this subject as the most complete. The Greeks said that human development involved the pursuit of four ideals— plenty, truth, good, and beauty. "Plenty" had to do with wealth. "Truth" spoke to the quest for knowledge and education. "Good" involved social or workplace justice, and "beauty" had to do with the search for both contentment and excitement.

This shift of emphasis from physical toward emotional security also allowed a shift from the conflict ethic toward a more cooperative one. Systems for increasing lower level employee participation in the making of decisions became increasingly popular. At the same time, a new participant was being invented, one that would introduce the post-Industrial Revolution. That participant was the computer/microprocessor. Technology had again become the key issue.

Traditionally, new technology has ultimately created new jobs. The microprocessor, however, with its ability to control entire processes, is proving different. The new jobs microprocessors create will also probably be handled by microprocessors. The computer is capable of solving a growing number of operational problems more efficiently than humans. If programmed correctly, it may be capable of producing even creative solutions. It is not, however, capable of defining its own purpose or of dealing effectively with the diverse range of constantly shifting variables in organizational social systems. These two responsibilities will remain the employee's in future management systems. The work environment will improve as more and more of the repetitious jobs are taken over. Educational levels will increase as technical demands grow. This same education will allow employees to define personal development in richer terms. It will encourage involvement in the transactional and contextual environments.

Rather than simply providing more jobs and plenty, therefore, the new technology is providing greater opportunity for overall development which includes but does not focus on the pursuit of plenty. "Plenty" is currently being seen less as an end in itself and more as a means which facilitates the pursuit of other ideals during non-working hours. This shift in attitude will provide at least a partial solution to the employee displacement problem. Consulting and job sharing, for example, will become increasingly attractive alternative life styles in the workplace.

Future, facilitating changes in organizational size/design will also be necessary. Because of the increasing expertise of lower level employees, hierarchies, as we have known them, are no longer functional. As a result of technological innovations, the large, centralized operation is also passe. Instead we will find loose networks of "experts" joined together mainly by technology. Organizational designs are being created to maintain the integrity of such networks, to link the involved freedom with direct bottom-line responsibility.

The new, more flexible organizations will, in turn, have to deal with shifting marketplace pressures. Because of changes in socio-economic thinking, status will be defined more in terms of content than image, more in terms of what people can do than what they can afford. Product usefulness will become an increasingly important criterion. Consumers will grow more selective. Fewer things will be bought mainly as showpieces. Value will depend on the ability of products and services to facilitate individual development.

The conflict ethic will also prove increasingly inefficient. The degree of waste in terms of both human and nonhuman resources will become unacceptable. A cooperative/competitive ethic will evolve in the internal environment of organizations. In the contextual environment major role changes will occur. The more efficient private sector will begin addressing social and environmental problems. Government will provide incentives and standards for such

135

efforts.

The cycle, therefore, at this point has completed itself twice. In many ways we have ended up back at the beginning. We are interested in emotional security again; emphasis is on cooperative problem solving; the cult of individualism is fading; what we can do is more important than what we have; businesses are being restructured to take fullest advantage of the expertise of all employees in decision making situations.

We are ready to start over and are looking for the appropriate vehicle. That vehicle is materializing as a result of our growing realization that neither the mechanical/quantitative nor the humanistic/qualitative schools of thought can win in their century long struggle for dominance. They are two sides of the same coin. Only by joining together can they make up the necessary whole.

The systems approach to management is the vehicle which allows us to bring the quantitative and qualitative frames of reference together. The systems approach says that "a whole is more than the sum of its parts." To understand an organization, to make it function effectively, one must take into account all involved systemic interactions — social, technical, and socio-technical — as well as the organization's relationship with the larger system/society of which it is a part. It must ask the "why" question as well as the "how." It must ask what role the organization can and should play in terms of its external as well as its internal community.

The systems approach to management, however, has eventually threatened too may players and been dismissed as yet another passing fad. It has been replaced by the quality improvement movement, which again calls for the integration of socio and technical systems to improve the quality of products, manufacturing processes, management systems, the work environment, and, finally, the external environment which indirectly affects productivity. Practitioners have quickly realized that in order to be effective, quality improvement efforts must become participative, wholistic, and on-going. In other words, they must become systemic.

Thus, we are embarking on our third cycle. The journey this time will probably be richer and more fulfilling due to all we have learned from previous struggles, though our evolutionary progress thus far has never been in a straight line. Rather, it has followed a circuitous, sometimes torturous path, trying many possible avenues before eventually leading us in the right direction. The fact remains, however, that we have come far, so far, in fact, that with this cycle we should finally be able to turn the historic corner alluded to earlier. We're definitely closing in on it. And to that I say amen...amen.

NOTES

1. Stafford Beer, Decision and Control, (New York: John Wiley and Sons, 1966), P. 92.

Bibliography

Ackoff, Russell. *Creating The Corporate Future.* New York: Wiley, 1981.

Ackoff, Russell. "Does Quality of Life Have to be Qualified?" *General Systems,* XX, 1975.

____. *Redesigning the Future,* New York: Wiley, 1974.

____. "Toward a System of Systems Concepts," *Management Science.* Vol. 3, No. 11, 1971.

Ackoff, Russell, and Emery, Fred. *On Purposeful Systems.* New York: Aldine Atherton, 1972.

Ackoff, Russell, and Vergara, Elsa. "Creativity in Problem Solving and Planning: A Review." *European Journal of Operations Research.* Vol. 7, 1981.

Allen, Kerry; Chaplin, Isolda; Keller, Shirley; and Hill, Donna. *Volunteers from the Workplace.* National Center of Voluntary Action, Washington, D.C., 1979.

Bannister, Robert C. *Social Darwinism: Science and Myth.* Philadelphia: Temple University Press, 1978.

Barnes, Norman. "Rethinking Corporate Charity." *Fortune Magazine.* October 1974.

Batter, William M. "Productivity and the Working Environment." The Wharton School of the University of Pennsylvania Dean's Lecture Series.

Beer, Stafford, *Decision and Control*. New York: Wiley, 1966.

Bennett, J., and Levine, S. "Industrialization and Social Deprivation," in *Japanese Industrialization and Its Social Consequences*, ed. Hugh Patrick. Berkeley: University of California Press, 1976.

Boriako, Allen. "The Chip" *National Geographic*. Vol. 162, No. 4, October 1982.

Boulding, K. *The Image*. Ann Arbor: University of Michigan Press, 1977.

Brom, Thomas. "The Parttime Job: A New Way of Life." Philadelphia *Bulletin*, December 3, 1978.

Brubacher, John S. *A History of the Problems of Education*. New York: McGraw-Hill, 1966.

Cardwell, D.S.L. *Turning Points in Western Technology*. New York: Neale Watson Academic Publications, 1972.

Cherns, Albert, and Davis, Louis. *The Quality of Working Life*. Vols. 1, 2. London: Collier Macmillan, 1975.

Churchman, West. *The Systems Approach*. New York: Delacorte Press, 1968.

Clutterbuck, David. "The Future of Work." *International Management*. August 1979.

Cohn, J.M., and Cohen, M.J. *The Penguin Dictionary of Modern Quotations*. Middlesex, England: Penguin Books, 1971.

Commoner, Barry. *The Closing Circle*. New York: Alfred A. Knopf, 1971.

"Company Courses Go Collegiate." *Business Week*. February 26, 1979.

Cooper, Michael; Gelfond, Peter; and Foley, Patricia. "Early Warning Signals– Growing Discontent Among Managers." *Business*. January-February 1980.

Dembart, Lee. "Expert Computers Raising Questions." Philadelphia *Inquirer*. Sunday, December 12, 1982.

Dickson, John. "Plight of Middle Management." *Management Today*. December 1977.

Ellul, Jacques. *The Technological Society*. New York: Vintage Books, 1967.

Emery, Fred. *Futures We Are In*. Leiden, The Netherlands: Martinus Nijhoff Social Sciences Division, 1977.

_____. *Systems Thinking*. Harmondsworth, England: Penguin Books, 1969.

_____. "The Fifth Wave? Embarking on the Next Forty Years." Unpublished, May 1978.

Emery, Fred, and Thorsrud, Einar. *Democracy at Work*. Leiden: Martinus Nijhoff Social Sciences Division, 1976.

Emery, Merrelyn. *Searching for New Directions in New Ways for New Times*. Canberra: Ontario Quality of Work Life Center, 1982.

Fenwick, P., and Lawler, E. "What You Really Want from Your Job." *Psychology Today.* May 1978.

Freeman, Alix. "Behind Every Successful Robot Is a Technician." *Careers '83.*

Fromm, Eric. *Escape from Freedom.* New York: Avon Books, 1941.

_____. "The Creative Attitude." In *Creativity and Its Cultivation,* ed. H. Anderson. London: Penguin Education, 1970.

Frost, D. "The Effects of Cooperation and Competition on the Creative Expression of College Students." *Dissertation Abstracts International.* Vol. 37 (7-A) 4229, January 1977.

Galenson, Walter, ed. *Comparative Labor Movements.* New York: Russell & Russell, 1952.

Galenson, Walter, and Lipset, Seymour. *Labor and Trade Unionism.* New York: Wiley, 1960.

George, Claude. *The History of Management Thought.* Englewood Cliffs, N.J.: Prentice-Hall, 1968.

Gharajedaghi, Jamshid. "On the Nature of Development." *Human Systems Management.* Vol. 4, 1984.

_____. "Organizational Implications of Systems Thinking: Multidimensional Modular Design." *European Journal of Operations Research.* August 1984.

Gilman, Robert. "Job Sharing Is Good." *The Co-Evolutionary Quarterly.* Spring 1978.

141

Ginzberg, Eli. "The Mechanization of Work." *Scientific American.*
September 1982.

Good, H.G. *A History of Western Education.* New York: Macmillan,
1947.

Guilford, J. "Traits of Creativity." In *Creativity and Its Cultivation,*
ed. H. Anderson. New York: Harper, 1959.

Guilano, Vincent. "The Mechanization of Office Work." *Scientific
American.* September 1982.

Gunn, Thomas. "The Mechanization of Design and Manufacturing."
Scientific American. September 1982.

Hackman, J. Richard, and Suttle, J. Lloyd. *Improving Life at Work.* Santa
Monica, Calif.: Goodyear Publishing, 1977.

Harrison, John B., and Sullivan, Richard E. *A Short History of Western
Civilization.* New York: Alfred A. Knopf, 1960.

Hodgson, Richard. "The death and Resurrection of Management
Teams." *The Business Quarterly.* Winter 1974.

Hofstadter, Douglas. "Metamagical Themas." *Scientific American.*
September 1982.

Holden, Constance. "Innovation: Japan Races Ahead as U.S. Falters."
Science. November 14, 1980.

Hoover, Wendell. "Springing the Creative Juices of Your
Committee." *Association Management.* Vol. 32, No. 4, April 1980.

Huddleston, Kenneth, and Fenwick, Dorothy. "The Productivity Challenge: Business/Education Partnership." *Training and Development Journal*. Vol. 37, No. 4, April 1983.

Hymowitz, Carol. "Employers Take Over Where Schools Fail to Teach the Basics." *Wall Street Journal*, January 22, 1981.

Jackson, K.F. *The Art of Solving Problems*. New York: St. Martin's Press, 1975.

Jardim, Anne. *The First Henry Ford*: A Study in Personality and Business Leadership. Cambridge, Mass.: MIT Press, 1970.

Jenkins, David. *Job Power*. Baltimore: Penguin Books, 1973.

Josephson, Matthew. *Robber Barons*. New York: Harcourt, Brace, 1934.

Katz, Daniel, and Kahn, Robert. *The Social Psychology of Organizations*. New York: Wiley, 1967.

Klemm, Frederick. *A History of Western Technology*. Cambridge, Mass.: MIT Press, 1954.

Koh, Andrew. "Interpreting Employee Needs: Assuming Versus Understanding." *Supervisor Management*. April 1981.

Krout, John A. *United States to 1865*. New York: Barnes & Noble 1955.

_____. *United States Since 1865*. New York: Barnes & Noble, 1955.

Leontief, Wassily. "The Distribution of Work and Income." *Scientific American.* September 1982.

Livingston, A.J. "The 80's: The Dangerous Decade." Philadelphia *Inquirer,* February 27-March 3, 1983.

Lohr, Steve. "Overhauling America's Business Management." *New York Times Magazine,* January 4, 1981.

Maslow, Abraham. *Motivation And Personality.* 2nd ed. New York: Harper and Row, 1970.

Miller, L. "Conflict: Facilitator or Inhibitor of Creative Performance?" *Dissertation Abstracts International.* Vol. 31 (7-B) 4316, January 1971.

Modern Systems Research for the Behavioral Scientist. Ed. Walter Buckley, Chicago: Aldine Press, 1965.

Murray, Thomas. "The Revolt of Middle Managers-Phase Two." *Dun's.* August 1973.

"New Breed of Workers." *U.S. News and World Report.* September 3, 1979.

Newell, A., and Simon, H. *Human Problem Solving.* Englewood Cliffs, N.J.: Prentice-Hall, 1972.

Oliver, John W. *History of American Technology.* New York: Ronald Press, 1956.

Osborn, Alex. *Applied Imagination.* New York: Scribner's, 1953.

Ozbekhan, Hasan. "Thoughts on the Emerging Methodology of Planning." The Wharton School, University of Pennsylvania.

_____. "Toward a General Theory of Planning." The Wharton School, University of Pennsylvania.

Parnes, S. J.; Noller, R.B.; and Biondi, A.M. *Guide to Creative Action.* New York: Scribner's, 1977.

Poincaré, H. "Mathematical Creation." In *Creativity,* ed. P. Vernon. London: Penguin Education, 1970.

Raina, M. "A Study Into the effects of Competition on Creativity." *Gifted Child Quarterly.* Vol. 12, No. 4, 1968.

Reich, Charles. *The Greening of America.* New York: Random House, 1970.

Reisner, Edward H. *The Evolution of the Common School.* New York: Macmillan, 1930.

Roe, A. "A Psychologist Examines Sixty-Four Eminent Scientists." In *Creativity,* ed. P. Vernon. London: Penguin Education, 1970.

Rogers, C. "Toward a Theory of Creativity." In *Creativity,* ed. P. Vernon. London: Penguin education, 1970.

Roth, William. *A Systems Approach to Quality Improvement.* New York: Praeger, 1992.

Roth, William. "Comparing the Effects of Cooperation, Competition, and Conflict on Speed With Which Different Personality Types and Personality Type Pairs Can Generate

145

Useful Solutions to Problems." Dissertation, University of Pennsylvania, 1982.

Roth, William. *Work and Rewards: Redefining Our Work-Life Reality*. New York: Praeger, 1989.

Roweton, W. "Creativity: A review of Theory and Research." Theoretical Paper No. 24. University of Wisconsin: Center for Cognitive Learning, March 1970.

Sachs, Ignacy. "The Conditions of Development: Whither Industrial Society?" Unpublished, June 1, 1978.

Schon, Donald. *Beyond the Stable State*. London: Temple Smith, 1971.

Selltiz, Claire, Wrightsman, Lawrence, and Cook, Stuart. *Research Methods in Social Relations*. 3rd Edition, New York: Holt, Reinehart and Winston, 1976.

"Some Lessons for the Decade Ahead: New Hand in the Workplace-The Robot." *U.S. News and World Report*. January 21, 1980.

The Quality of Working Life, Vol. 2. Ed. Louis E. Davis, Albert B. Cherns. London: The Free Press, 1975.

The Relevance of General Systems Theory. Ed. Ervin Laszlo. New York: George Braziller, 1978.

"The Vision of MITI Policies in the 1980's." Ministry of International Trade and Industry, Tokyo.

Toffler, Alvin. *Future Shock*. New York: Random House, 1970.

Trist, Eric. "The Evolution of Socio-Technical Systems." *Issues in the Quality of Working Life.* No. 2. Ontario: Ontario Ministry of Labor, 1980.

____. "The Quality of Working Life and Organizational Improvement." Unpublished, Management and Behavioral Science Center, The Wharton School, October 1979.

Trist, Eric; Higgins, G.W.; Murray, H.; and Pollock, A.B. *Organizational Choice.* London: Tavistock Publications, 1963.

Vogel, E. "Toward More Accurate Concepts." In *Modern Japanese Organization and Decision Making,* ed. E. Vogel. Berkeley: University of California Press, 1975.

Vogel, R. "The Effects of Experimentally Induced Conflict on Creativity Activity." *Dissertations Abstracts.* Vol. 29 (7-B) 2661, July 1969.

Von Bertalanffy, Ludwig. "General Systems Theory, A Critical Review." *General Systems.* Vol. VII, 1962.

Weber, Eugene. *The Western Tradition from the Renaissance to the Atomic Age.* University of California, Los Angeles: D.C. Heath, 1965.

Wells, H.G. *The Outline of History.* Garden City, N.Y.: Garden City Books, 1949.

Westerman, Jewell. "Look Who's Covered in red Tape." *Fortune.* May 4, 1981.

INDEX

FOR ADDITIONAL COPIES OF
THE EVOLUTION OF MANAGEMENT THEORY

Mail this form to: Wm. Roth & Associates
                        6223 Hilltop Road
                        Orefield, PA 18069

Please send me _____ copies of the book at $11.95 per copy
for a total of _____ (checks payable to: WM. ROTH & ASSOCIATES)

Name (Please Print) _____

Address _____

City _____ State _____ Zip _____

My phone number is _____ My FAX is _____

    For institutional orders of more than 10 copies call (215) 395-3449 or FAX (215) 395-3604 for special instructions and discount information.

Thank You